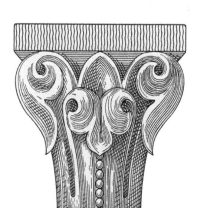

The
Dark   Secret
of
G:.A:.O:.T:.U:.

Dr. Ana Méndez Ferrell

The Dark Secret of G:.A:.O:.T:.U:.

Dr. Ana Méndez Ferrell

The Dark Secret of G:.A:.O:.T:. U:.
© 2010 Dr. Ana Méndez Ferrell.
1st English Edition, 3rd Print 2018

Original Spanish Title: El Oscuro Secreto de G:.A:.D:.U:.

All Scripture quotations, unless otherwise indicated, are taken from *NIV - New International Version of the Bible.*

Category: Deliverance

Publisher:
Voice Of The Light Ministries
P. O. Box 3418
Ponte Vedra, FL. 32004
United States of America

www.VoiceOfTheLight.com

ISBN13: 978-1-944681-21-0

I dedicate this book to the only true God, Jehova of the Armies, to Jesus Christ His Son, and to the Holy Spirit. I also dedicate it to Tanya Warldorff, without whose help and courage, the execution of this manuscript would not have been possible.

TABLE OF CONTENTS

AN IMPORTANT WORD FROM THE AUTHOR

Masonry professes to respect all the religious creeds with ample tolerance. It claims to be a universal instrument of brotherhood and benevolence; a chain of love, wisdom, and good habits which fraternize the world.

Perhaps you, dear reader, love God with all your heart, or maybe you have undergone the marvelous experience of making Jesus Christ your Lord and Savior. Maybe you think that Masonry does not oppose the One True God and that you may practice your faith and frequently attend your Masonic Lodge without any consequence. If this is true and GAOTU, the Great Architect of the Universe is the true God, then you are not at any risk. But, if it were possible to reveal the dark hidden secret, which the highest degrees conceal with such zeal, that Freemasonry is an overt cult to Satan, then this is the most important book that has ever fallen into your hands.

If you are not a religious man, but somebody who is in search of the fundamental answers to life and this caused your initiation into such an order, this book will help you find Truth and it will give you answers to many queries found within you.

Maybe you are neither one nor the other, but somebody seeking to know what lurks behind this secret society because somebody in your family is involved in it. You have realized there is something affecting your life, and you have a feeling that Masonry may be responsible for it. You will not be disappointed. In these pages, you will discover and understand things you never ever imagined.

Throughout this book, you will be taken through a profound and sobering study of the secrets and hidden depths of Masonry. To do this, we have meticulously researched numerous documents in order to obtain the utmost faithfulness and truthfulness underlying the conclusions stated in this book.

Amongst the many sources of documentaries, we have based our findings on the original Manuals of the Rites of the Order, up to the 33rd degree; on the books edited by Sovereign Grand Inspector Generals from the officers of Scottish Freemasonry and on those from the Grand Orient of France; on original documents from the worldwide Masonry Conferences; on reputable historians and politicians who have seen themselves involved with this "August Association"; and on veritable Testimonies from Masons and ex-Masons who have exposed their lives so you can learn the truth.

More than a simple book, it's an exposé in which you will discover the horrors of what Masonry is capable of, and of the extreme danger faced by those who are found among its ranks. Unfortunately, it's not only those directly connected to the Order that endure great suffering and misfortune of every sort, but also all their descendants. I myself was a victim of very strong curses, which I did not know how to put an end to, until I discovered that their origin came from

Masonry. My grandfather had been part of this organization and the evil affliction did not end when he died. There was a generational legacy that needed to be dealt with.

Just like me, many, many people, more than we can imagine, are suffering the consequences of having had someone in their family who has been part of this secret society.

This is a book that will fill you with the necessary light to open your eyes, to understand and to find the answers that will take you to full liberty.

A great amount of time, courage and risk have been invested to reveal all the hidden truths recounted in all their crudeness. It is up to you to analyze and weigh them using your faculties of full reasoning, along with the fear of God, which guards every man in the principles of Wisdom.

CHAPTER

FREEMASONRY UNCOVERED

Masonry or Freemasonry is the most widespread secret society worldwide and has the greatest historical tradition.

Freemasonry is a fraternal organization that arose from obscure origins in the late 16th to early 17th century. Freemasonry now exists in various forms all over the world, with a membership estimated at around 5 million, including just under two million in the United States and around 480,000 in England, Scotland and Ireland. The various forms all share moral and metaphysical ideals, which include, in most cases, a constitutional declaration of belief in a Supreme Being.[1] In its inception, Masonry was a society that grouped cathedral builders from the Middle Ages. These craftsmen had certain privileges and were called Franc-maçons (literally "Free Masons"), a denomination that gave rise to the synonyms Masonry and Freemasonry. With the decline of cathedral building in Europe, the groups, or "Lodges" in Masonry terminology, began admitting into its organization, people not connected to this activity.

The society transformed and began acquiring an ideological and symbolic content. During the 17'th and 18'th centuries, they adopted some religious rites mainly from the old orders of Chivalry. They took Hiram Abiff's persona as an inspiration, since he was one of the greatest metalworkers and craftsmen in charge of building Solomon's Temple. In the chapters to come, This character's true occult identity will be revealed. For the common Mason, Hiram Abiff is just the architect of the building erected for God by the Hebrew King, but for the elite members of the organization, it is something much deeper.

The Masonic society was well accepted by civil and religious people in certain countries, but met great opposition from the Roman Catholic Church. They have continually declared since 1738, that any of its parishioners who joins with this fraternity becomes guilty of a serious sin and must therefore be excommunicated. The main reason for this attitude is that Catholicism considers Masonry to be "The Devil's Party" due to the fearsome satanic ceremonies contained therein.

Despite this statute, many of the Catholic church's high ranking members clandestinely adhered to the forbidden society. Freemasonry teachings are far from being congruent with the original Christianity we find in the Bible. Instead, many of them are, what is known today as, "New Age". All religions are joined together in Masonry, as well as Humanism, Deism and Naturalism. For this reason, it is not surprising that in 1990, one of the official Masonic publications in North America was named "THE NEW AGE."

The famous Spanish historian Ricardo de la Cierva[2], in one of his books, "Enigmas in History I", mentions a Jesuit, Father José Antonio Ferrer. He was a professor at the University of Zaragoza who had been commissioned by the University to study Masonry in depth. In this book, De la Cierva refers to a speech Father Ferrer gave where he professes that religious members, priests, and bishops were involved in Masonry. He alleges that there were more than two thousand Masonic clergymen in the 18'th century and lodges had even been founded inside convents. It is now known that several of the representatives of traditional Protestant and Evangelical churches around the world are amongst its ranks and many occupy high Masonry degrees.

I attribute this power of seduction, with which Masonry has been able to entangle so many Evangelicals and Clergy, to the subliminal and fraudulent manner in which they impart their doctrine to the initial degrees (the first three). These new followers totally ignore the depths of the Order and its darkest secret. For them, it is a fraternity centered on the well being of the family, an organization with a philanthropic character, and a grouping of people with political and financial interests.   However, they do not fail to acknowledge the strange and even frightening character of the rites. Terrible truths are zealously guarded and I intend to bring them to light so the genuine intentions of this secret society can be discerned with clarity.

From its beginnings, the power of Freemasonry was extraordinary and it quickly spread out among the aristocracy, politicians and high society. Between 1737 and 1907, sixteen English princes have belonged to the order. Contained in the list of previous Grand Masters, we find George IV, Edward VII, Edward VIII and George V of England; Oscar II and Gustav V of Sweden, and Frederick VIII and Christian X of Denmark. In modern times, we find Francois Mitterrand, ex-president of France, who was Grand Master Inspector General of the Great Orient of France in 1962 and 1969. On August 5th, 1981, Time Magazine published an article that listed seventeen presidents of the United States as having been Masons. On this list we find Gerald Ford, Jimmy Carter, George Bush, G.W Bush as well as prominent figures of worldwide influence such as David Rockefeller and Henry Kissinger. This magazine included in its list, Carlos Andres Perez, ex-president of Venezuela and Omar Torrijos, Panama's, now deceased, ex-dictator.

Also known in this circle as great predecessors of Freemasonry, was none other than George Washington, Benjamin Franklin and, in Mexico, Benito Juarez.

Walt Disney is the founder of the Walt Disney Company.

Left: Benito Juarez was the President of Mexico. (1858-1872) 33rd Degree Mason.
Right: Henry Kissinger 33rd Degree Mason. He was the Secretary of State in United
States and worked in the Richard Nixon and Gerald Ford administrations among other
important positions in American politics.

A large number of presidents and leaders in the world have belonged to this "Secret Society".

Although Freemasonry is in itself "A Great Fraternity" worldwide, it has divided into different branches. The most important ones are "The Old and Accepted Scottish Rite" and "The York Rite". (See all the institutions and branches in Appendix 1). It must be understood that the "Scottish Rite" does not bear this name because it originated in Scotland. It was actually the name given to the American adaptation of the "Rite of Perfection" from the French Freemasonry.

In France, two separate societies are based on the "Scottish Rite" under the name of SUPREME COUNCIL or "Supreme Power of Masonic Order" and the THE GREAT ORIENT OF FRANCE, or "Great College of all Freemasonic Rites". Each one issues their own identifications and degrees. A Rite is made up of a succession of degrees, conferred by one or various established bodies, but under the authority of one supreme government.

Adam Weishaupt[3], founder of the order of "The Illuminati", was determined to infiltrate the continental branch of Freemasonry and by 1782, his goal was achieved at the International Masonic Convention of Wilhelmsbad, Germany.

Adam felt that human society had grown hopelessly corrupt and that it could only be saved by a complete overhaul.

George Washington. A military man who was the first President of The United States (1789-1797) and Commander of the Continental Army of the revolutionary forces during the United States War of Independence. (1775-1783)

In effect, he was the first utopian to think on a global scale(3), and he looked forward to the day his group would bring about the Novus Ordo Seclorum, sometimes called the New World Order.

Weishaupt, who was indoctrinated in Egyptian occultism, developed a five-year plan to join all occult systems into one powerful, secret organization. Among Weishaupt's goals were:

1. The abolition of the monarchy and established governments.
2. The abolition of private property and inheritance.
3. The abolition of patriotism and nationalism.
4. The abolition of family life and the institution of marriage; and the establishment of communes for elementary education.
5. The abolition of all religions.

All of this doctrine being revealed, which makes one shudder, will be expanded on in subsequent chapters, as we study the different degrees, and especially, degree 33.

In 1978, Professor John Robinson[4], a highly respected British historian and longtime Mason, wrote in his book, Proof of a Conspiracy:

"I have discovered that the secret shell of the Masonic Lodges has been used in every country to ventilate and to propagate political and religious sentiments that could not have been exposed to the outside without having put to risk the author to serious dangers. I have observed how these doctrines have been disseminating and mixing with the different Freemasonry systems, until finally an organization has formed with the express purpose of uprooting all established religion and to distort all existing governments in Europe." While investigating the writings of a former Mason, Count Virieu, I read how he expressed his dismay, when referring to this infiltration and used these spine-chilling words:

"I will not confide them to you. I can only tell you that all this is very much more serious than you think. The conspiracy which is being woven is so well thought out, that it will be, so to speak, impossible for the Monarchy and the Church to escape it."

According to his biographer, Costa de Beauregard, De Virieu denounced the Illuminati and became a devout Catholic from that time until his death. De Beauregard wrote:

"the Comte de Virieu could only speak of Freemasonry with horror."

Weishaupt encouraged people to join the brotherhood, promising them power, influence and success in the world. At the same time, it was assured that members would feel totally committed and bound to it through the organization obtaining reports of a "sensitive nature" about their personal lives. Sometimes they were even involved in crimes with the promise that nobody could touch them as long as they belonged to the Order. Weishaupt wrote:

"The pupils are convinced that the Order will rule the world. Every member therefore becomes a ruler. We all think of ourselves as qualified to rule. It is therefore an alluring thought both to good and bad men. Therefore the Order will spread."

"Are you sufficiently aware what ruling means, to rule in a secret society? Not only over the smallest and the greatest of the population, but over the best men, men of every level of society, of every nation and every religion. To rule without any external force, indissolubly united; breathing a same spirit and a same feeling in them, men distributed throughout the face of the earth."

Weishaupt also urged his followers not to shy away from committing acts of violence or to commit crimes advancing Illuminati objectives. He wrote:

"Sin is only that which is hurtful, and if the profit is greater than the damage, it becomes a virtue."

This is, of course, a simple reformulation of the wicked Illuminati shibboleth, "the end justifies the means."

Here is a passage taken from a well known Freemason forum speaking about one of the most prominent satanists that ever existed, Alister Crowley[5]:

"Consequently like every human who ever walked this Earth, Crowley made mistakes ... big mistakes. But in delving into the inner secrets of Gnosticism he unearthed the true nature of Gnosis, **the Dark Initiates** who control most of the **Secret Societies** and also the non-human intelligence, the **Dark Gods**, behind it all."

Crowley has been grossly abused since his death by people who wish to denigrate his name and work or pervert his work for their own ends; these are the very same people who are inheritors of Weishaupt's subversive cult, the Illuminati. These are the **Black Adepts of the Cult of Evil, the Secret Masters of the Dark Empire of Secret Societies** who are the true **Lords of Power on Earth** that have taken command of Freemasonry and all other cults of note or influence.

Subversive and irreligious as each of these disparate societies was in its own right, now they were united to the body of Illuminized Freemasonry and had produced a weapon of terrifying potency with which to attack Moral and Civic Order. As is the want of traitors and subversives, those at the meeting were obliged not to reveal anything on oath. Francois Henri de Virieu (1754-93), an attendee at the conference, who was a Freemason from the Martiniste Lodge at Lyons, upon his return home, when questioned about the Congress, and the "tragic secrets" he said he knew, answered:

"Deluded people; you must understand that there exists a Conspiracy in favor of despotism and against liberty, incapacity against talent, of vice against virtue, of ignorance against light! It is formed in the depths of the most impenetrable darkness, a society is to rule the world, to appropriate the authority of sovereigns, to usurp their place . . . Every species of error which afflicts the earth, every half-baked idea, every invention serves to fit the doctrines of the Illuminati . . . I see that all great fundamentals which society has made good use of to retain the allegiance of man - such as religion and law - will be without power to destroy an organization which has made itself a cult, and put itself above all human legislation.

Finally, I see the release of calamities whose end will be lost in the night of ages, activities devours the entrails of the globe and escapes into the air with a violent and devastating explosion."

A fellow Frenchman and Freemason, the Marquis de Luchet (1739-92) confirmed de Virieu's warning of the terrors planned for France by the Illuminati.

The Freemason Forum continues saying[6]:

Historians have never understood the real purpose of this terrible congress and the effects of this merger between Illuminism and Freemasonry on the history of the world. Weishaupt's success in allying Illuminism and Freemasonry has been of the darkest significance for the world. For this concordat had not only joined together all the leading secret societies of the day and united "not less than three million members all over the world" but it had opened the way for the **Dark Adepts** to infiltrate and take control of these secret organizations. And then to bring these disparate organizations together in a seamless whole that had one ultimate aim, even though the vast majority of the initiates within the Lodges did not know it, which was world domination by **the Elect**, the **secret Brotherhood of Darkness.**

These are the Occult Hierarchy that is the Ancient **Luciferian Priesthood** who can claim an ancient lineage of service to evil going far back in history, back before recorded history began. These few men, intergenerational Satanists and Luciferians are the true leaders of the Illuminati for they are the **Secret Masters of the dark Empire of Secret Societies** and the true **Lords of Power on Earth."** Manly P. Hall, was a very famous occult and mystic writer and a powerful mason. He wrote, describing the core belief of Freemasonry, the New Age Movement and the coming **One World Religion**:

"... When the Mason learns that the key to the warrior on the block is the proper application of the dynamo of living power, he has learned the mystery of his Craft. The seething energies of Lucifer are in his hands and before he may step onward and upward, he must prove his ability to properly apply energy."

"The true Mason is not creed-bound. He realizes with the divine illumination of his Lodge that as a Mason his religion must be universal: **Christ, Buddha or Mohammed, the name means little, for he recognizes only the light and not the bearer. He worships at every shrine, bows**

before every altar, whether in temple, mosque or cathedral, realizing with his truer understanding the oneness of all spiritual truth. No true Mason can be narrow, for his Lodge is the divine expression of all broadness."

"A Mason is not appointed; he is evolved and he must realize that the position he holds in the exoteric Lodge means nothing compared to his position in the spiritual Lodge of life ... and that his Masonic rites must eternally be speculative until he makes them operative by living the life of the mystic Mason..."

"The Masonic order is not a mere social organization, but is composed of all those who have banded themselves together to learn and apply the principles of mysticism and the occult rites."

"The Mason believes in the Great Architect, the living keystone of creation's plan, the Master of all Lodges, without whose spirit there is no work. Let him never forget that the Master is near. Day and night let him feel the presence of the Supreme or Overshadowing One. The All-Seeing Eye is upon him. Day and night this great Orb measures his depths, seeing into his innermost soul of souls, judging his life, reading his thoughts, measuring his aspirations, and rewarding his sincerity. To this All-Seeing One he is accountable; to none other must he account. This Spirit passes with him out of the Lodge and measures the Mason in the world."

Among the many Freemasonry sources, it is also important to analyze the writings of Albert Pike. His teachings and dogma from the ancient and accepted "Scottish Rites" of Freemasonry were first published in 1871 and returned to the mainstream when they were again published in 1966.

Albert Pike

Supposedly, they were to be used exclusively by the Council of those who had reached the 33rd degree. Pike was probably the most prominent exponent of the Masonic creed and doctrine and he was the Sovereign Grand Commander of "The Supreme Council" who gave birth to all of the Supreme Councils of the World. He is known among his followers as the "Pope of Freemasonry".

Let's not forget that Weishaupt learned the rituals of the occult ceremonies from the Egyptians and therefore, symbolism plays an important role in this Rite.

Without further comment, I will cite some excerpts from the 1966 edition of Morals and Dogma of the Ancient and Accepted Scottish Rite of Freemasonry, or Rite of Perfection, written by the leader of Freemasonry in North America, Albert Pike.

In Morals and Dogma, Pike wrote:

"Masonry, like all the Religions, all the Mysteries, Hermeticism and Alchemy, conceals its secrets from all except the Adepts and Sages, or the Elect, and uses false explanations and misinterpretations of its symbols to mislead those who deserve only to be misled; to conceal the Truth, which it calls Light, from them, and to draw them away from it. Truth is not for those who are unworthy or unable to receive it, or would pervert it.... (pg. 104, 105)

The truth must be kept secret, and the masses need a teaching proportioned to their imperfect reason...

...every man's conception of God must be proportioned to his mental cultivation and intellectual powers, and moral excellence. God is, as man conceives Him, the reflected image of man himself..."[7]

This next statement reduces the Masonic philosophy to a single premise. Pike writes:

"The true name of Satan, the Kabalists say, is that of Yahveh reversed; for Satan is not a black god but the negation of God. The Devil is the personification of Atheism or Idolatry.

Lucifer, the Light Bearer! Strange and mysterious name to

give to the Spirit of Darkness! Lucifer, the Son of the Morning! Is it he who bears the Light and with its splendors intolerable blinds feeble, sensual or selfish Souls?

Doubt it not!" [8]

Here, Albert Pike explains in Morals & Dogma how the true nature of Freemasonry is kept a secret from Masons of lower degrees:

"The Blue Degrees are but the outer court or portico of the Temple. Part of the symbols are displayed there to the Initiate, but he is intentionally misled by false interpretations. It is not intended that he shall understand them; but it is intended that he shall imagine he understands them. Their true explication is reserved for the Adepts, the Princes of Masonry. The whole body of the Royal and Sacerdotal Art was hidden so carefully, centuries since, in the High Degrees, as that it is even yet impossible to solve many of the enigmas which they contain. It is well enough for the mass of those called Masons, to imagine that all is contained in the Blue Degrees; and whoso attempts to undeceive them will labor in vain, and without any true reward violate his obligations as an Adept. Masonry is the veritable Sphinx, buried to the head in the sands heaped round it by the ages."[9]

Key phrases that Pike also wrote in Morals and Dogma:
"Each Masonic temple is a religious temple" (pg. 213).

"The first Masonic legislator was .... Buddha" (pg. 277).

"Freemasonry, in which Christian, Hebrew, Muslim and Brahman altars are raised, where followers of Confucius of Krishna and Zoroastrian believers can gather, bond and join their prayers to the only God who is above all the Baals" (pg. 226).

"All of the scientific, and grandiose from the religious dreams of the "Illuminati"... have been taken from Kabbalah; all Masonic associations owe to this one, all their secrets and their symbols." (Pg. 744). (The Kabala or Kabbalah is the occult and mystic philosophy behind Judaism).

Many enter Freemasonry seeking God through its enigmatic traditions, believing Him to be so unreachable that it is only possible for a few to obtain the level necessary. Others, enter seeking to build relationships with important people. They disregard what they don't understand in their rites to the ends of obtaining power through influential contacts.

These people see Lodges as a kind of exclusive social club. Others, blinded by greed and power, are initiated to receive the extraordinary Masonic assistance and therefore, reach their highest satisfaction of success. Still, there are others who groom themselves because they want to develop their ego to its full potential and use the power of the mind to control their peers. Unfortunately, what they all have in common is that they join without knowing the true aim of this association and are totally blinded to the spiritual powers that rule over it. Whether we admit it or not, there are spiritual forces at work. Though we may not take them into account, or even deny their existence, it doesn't prevent them from having an influence over our lives. In many cases, these forces drag their naïve victims into the depths of depression, to insanity and even unto death.

My intention is to unmask the secrets and the deep pits of Freemasonry in order to shed a true light for those who have a sincere heart and are searching for God, or for those who believe they have a relationship with Him. I want to offer a way out to all who want to escape from the ties of Freemasonry and occultism and its inevitable and terrible eternal destiny.

As King Solomon said:

"There is a way that seems right to a man, but in the end it leads to death."   *Proverbs 16:25*

The Bible is the Sacred Book of Freemasonry. In most of the "Rites," it appears deposited upon "The Ara". (The Masonic altar) and remains continually open as a symbol of divine wisdom. For this reason, I will  refer to it as the starting point so that we can get to the truth of who God truly is, what His Personality and His thought-life are, and based on His teachings, be able to analyze the deceit of Freemasonry.

Although I am going to use the names Jehovah or Yahweh and Jesus Christ's, and likewise, the principles established by them, this does not mean I will be referring to any particular religion. I will simply be emphasizing the scriptural foundation therein contained.

The Occult, in whichever of its forms, brings serious consequences to those who practice it. The spiritual world is a dangerous terrain lest it is entered through the right door. Not everything that glitters is gold, and not every light comes from God.

*"...Before I go to the place of no return, to the land of gloom and deep shadow, to the land of deepest night, of deep shadow and disorder. The land of sunless gloom as intense darkness, [the land] of the shadow of death, without any order, and where **the light is as thick darkness."*** Job 10:21-22*

"Give glory to the Lord your God before he brings the darkness, before your feet stumble on the darkening hills. You hope for light, but he will turn it to thick darkness and change it to deep gloom."
Jeremiah 13:16

In the chapters to follow, we will see how Freemasonry brings terrible curses upon a person and their descendants. Even people who have left it, are still bound to constant misfortune. The important thing to realize, is that one can get out and be set free of its bondage.

Notes

1. Wikkipedia

2. De la Cierva, Ricardo: Enigmas in History I, Editor Fenix. 2003, pg. 264. (Original Spanish Title: Enigmas de la Historia)

3. Weishaupt, Adam: founder of the order of "The Illuminati" (a secret association that intends to unite the most powerful and illuminated men in the world).

4. Robinson, John: Proof of Conspiracy, 4 Ed. New York, 1798, pg. 134.

5. www.overlordsofchaos.com

6. The Lost Keys of Freemasonry (1923) at

http://www.overlordsofchaos.com/html/illuminati.html

7. Albert Pike: Morals and Dogma, Chapter 3 pg. 104, 105 online

8. Albert Pike: Morals and Dogma, pg. 172 online

9. Albert Pike: Morals and Dogma, pg. 819 online

Be aware that there are two distinct different versions of the book: The original manuscript published in 1871 with subsequent reprint (hard to find) and a reprint from circa 2000 (Volume one ISBN #0766126152 Volume two ISBN: 0766126161). There is evidence to suggest that some wording has been changed in the more recent reprint, so all serious researchers should look for a 'library binding' published prior to 1950.

An online version of Morals and Dogma can be found at the Pietre- Stones Review of Freemasonry site, and is highly recommended if you wish to confirm the accuracy of quotes used on the ThreeWorldWars site.

CHAPTER

THE PRINCIPLES OF DEITY

1.- The Need for Epistemology

Epistemology is the doctrine of fundamentals and methodology behind all scientific knowledge. **In other words, how do we know that we know.**

Since his origin, man's search has been to find the answers to his own existence. Who are we? Where did we come from? Where are we going? What is the reason for our existence? What's after death? Philosophers of every age have tried to find a solution and have come up with hundreds of answers to these questions.

I take for granted the absolute certainty of the existence of a Supreme God over this marvelous and surprising Creation, given one cannot be a Mason lest one believes in some god. I will not address the theory of atheism because it is not the purpose of this book. From my point of view, it is a theory that falls on its own, since I consider it impossible for an organized universe, with life possessing such a high level of complexity, which may have come into existence by atoms that joined together by random happenstance.

Therefore, we will try to reach a conclusion from the only two reasonable possibilities in this case, Deism or a personal God.

A. Deism

A philosophy according to which everything comes from an impersonal God who is nothing else but cosmic energy, manifesting itself in the dimensions of visible matter and of the invisible realm of the spirit. For deists, "the all" is composed from an architectural master blueprint that diversifies into a multiplicity of parallel planes. A macrocosm and a microcosm connected by a flow of pure energy that makes existence possible.

It is a universe where nothing is lost and everything is transformed, where every living organism evolves until it reaches the absolute perfection of spirit and matter. This is the conceptualization of the universe currently held in the 21'st century, to a great extent, from the Western world-view which originates in the Eastern cultures. It is this type of thinking that we find in the Masonic writings and that allows all gods to be represented under one name: The Great Architect of the Universe. G:.A:.O:.T:.U:.

B. Everything Comes from a Personal God

God conceived, loved and gave form to His creation. This is the Judeo-Christian concept of the origin and of the finality of all things.

If we analyze the first theory, we will encounter a serious problem, it becomes highly improbable that creatures with personality can be derived from the abstract energy of an impersonal universe. There is no possible explanation as to where personality comes from. This is what gives Human beings the special characteristics that makes them unique and different on Earth. From this stance, Man will never, ever be able to answer his own questions, "Who am I?," "Where do I come from?" .

Man thinks and communicates his reasoning through the spoken and the written word. Man is capable of loving and of hating, of suffering and of rejoicing, is capable of feeling guilt or remorse, has an innate moral conscience and is undeniably creative. All of these attributes are impossible to explain through an impersonal universe, or from an alchemic formula for the transmutation of elements.

The second theory is much more weighty for, if I see

myself as a being who thinks, loves, creates, laughs, hurts, has a moral conscience, etc., it stands to reason that my creator inevitably must have, at the very least, the attributes I have. And if among them, is my capacity to relate to my peers, it's easy to arrive at the conclusion that God Himself, is also the creator of relationships. Therefore, a continuous flow of communication exists between the Creator and his creatures. With many, the Judeo-Christian concept is the one, which offers the most consistent answers to our existential dilemma.

It is important to acknowledge that we need faith to believe in any form of God. Also, to believe in any theory about the formation of the universe, requires faith as well. While I was gathering the documentation to draw the conclusions over which I've based this book, I read the most incredible theories about the origin of our universe and of man, written by atheist scientists, thinkers, gods, avatars, illuminated ones, etc. In the end, all the theories mentioned required faith. None of them were verifiable, given that not even the "scientific" theory of evolution can be proven, as Darwin himself confessed.

At least in my case, I need much more faith to imagine how one afternoon a reptile motivated himself to look up at the sky and decided he needed to fly, until one day, just like that, without any explanation, its cells began to change and wings sprung forth, along with the understanding of aerodynamics. If this were true, how is it possible that man has never achieved this metamorphosis being infinitely more intelligent than a reptile? It is easier to believe in an Almighty God who said: "let there be birds in the sky " and thus they were made. Or, as is stated in the Book of Hebrews in the Bible:

"By faith we understand that the universe was formed at God's command, so that what is seen was not made out of what was visible."   *Hebrews 11:3*

In a magnificent explanation about what faith is, the famous Swiss theologian, Francis Schaffer, said something to this effect:

"One must analyze the word faith and see that it can mean two completely opposite things. Suppose we are climbing in the Alps and are very high on the bare rock and suddenly the fog rolls in. The guide turns to us and says that the ice is forming and that there is no hope of descending before we will all freeze to death here on the exposed slope of the mountain.

Simply to keep warm, the guide keeps us moving in the dense fog further out on the edge until none of us have any idea where we are. After an hour or so, someone says to the guide: "suppose I dropped and hit a ledge ten feet down in the fog. What would happen then?" The guide would say that you might make it till the morning and live. So with absolutely no knowledge, or any reason to support the action, one member of the group hangs and drops into the fog. This would be one kind of faith, a leap of faith. Suppose however, after we have worked our way out on the edge, in the mist of the fog and the growing ice on the rock, we have stopped and we heard a voice who said, "you cannot see me, but I know exactly where you are from your voices. I am on another ridge. I have lived in these mountains, man and boy, for over sixty years and I know every foot of them. I can assure you that ten feet below you there s a ledge. If you hang and drop, you can make it through the night and I will get you in the morning.

I would not hang and drop at once, but would ask questions to try to ascertain if the man knew what he was talking about and if he was not my enemy. In the Alps, for example, I would ask him his name. If the name he gave me was the name of a family from that part of the mountains, it would count a great deal to me. In the Swiss alps, there are certain family names that indicate mountain families of the area. For example, in the area of the Alps where I live, Avanthey would be such a name. In my desperate situation, even though time would be running out, I would ask him, what to me, would be the sufficient questions and when I became convinced of the answers, then I would hang and drop.

This is faith, but obviously it has no relationship to the first instance. As a matter of fact, if one should be called faith, the other should not be designated with the same word representation. The historic Christian faith, is not a leap of faith in the post-kierkegaardian sence, because "He is not silent" and I am invited to ask the sufficient questions in regard to details, but also in regard to the existence of the universe and its complexity and in regard to the existence of man." [1]

In both cases of this short story, faith was required to make a decision, but for the second one, it was not about "blind" faith. Rather, it was based on the security that came from the voice giving direction. Likewise, we need faith to believe in reincarnation, in transmutation of elements, in the existence of Nirvana (paradisiacal spiritual state in Eastern religions), in Darwin's evolution, in the alchemic creation of Hermes Trismegistus, or in the Genesis of the Bible and in the personal God Who created all things.

The important thing is not the philosophic, or religious story that prevails in a given culture, or in a fraternity such as Freemasonry, but having certainty of whose voice is behind that Doctrine.

2.-Ecumenism

The basis for ecumenical thought is centered specifically on the existence of one single God, "Creator of the universe" and it is man, through different cultures and religions, who has given Him different names. This means that for Ecumenicals, Allah, Jehovah, Brahma, Dalai Lama, etc., are all the same God. For them, all roads lead to God and believing and seeking this, is the path to the peace and unity in the world we so desire. This philosophy, which has unquestionable charm, eliminates the God of the Bible by equating Him to a level of parity to all the rest of the "gods."

Let's keep in mind what He says of Himself:

"Fear ye not, neither be afraid: have not I told thee from that time, and have declared it? Ye are even my witnesses. Is there a God beside me? Yea, there is no God; I know not any."   Isaiah 44:8

Differing from the descriptions of other gods, Jehovah, or Yahweh, as He names Himself, is a God uniquely in three persons. The book of Genesis begins by saying:

"In the beginning God created the heavens and the earth."   Genesis 1:1

In the original Hebrew writings, the verb is in the singular, however, the word God is Elohim, which is the word for "Authorities", in the plural. This indicates the plurality inside the oneness of the Deity: God the Father, God the Son and God the Holy Spirit.

The account in Genesis continues further on stating:

"Then God said, Let us make man in our image, in our likeness...So God created man in his own image, in the image of God created he him."   Genesis 1:26, 27

In this passage we also see how God talks about Himself as referring to the persons who compose the trinity. The Bible verses demonstrating that Jesus is God are innumerable; that He is the Trinity's second person; that He became incarnated and was made man. His very name, announced by the archangel Gabriel means, *"God with us" (Emanuel), and Jesus means "Jehovah saves" (Isaiah 9:6 and Luke 1:31).*

In occult philosophies, as is in almost every religion, we find a great number of trinities and trilogies, which are quite different from the biblical Trinity. The basic trinity these religions possess is founded in a concept of various gods, who form a divine family made up of father, mother and son. For example, in Egypt we encounter Osiris (the father), Isis (the mother) and Horus (the son). Within the Babylonian structure there is Nimrod, Semiramis and Tamuz. This model carries over to other cultures and is a polytheistic concept; given each one of the parties in these trilogies is a different god. In contrast, the God of the Bible is the Sole God who manifests Himself in three distinct persons and none of them is mother. Neither, do we find in the Bible that God condones the worship of any spiritual entity having the figure of mother. In Roman Catholicism and in the Orthodox Church, the Virgin Mary is given a preeminent place in their services, but that doesn't mean it is God, nor a part of the Trinity.

Freemasonry, joins all gods together simply by identifying them with the number three. Based on the harmless number "three", the initiate accepts without any difficulty, this extremely dangerous symbiosis among divinities.

Here is an example of, how God sees this manner of thinking, which mixes one god with another as if they were the same.

"I marvel that ye are so soon removed from him that called you into the grace of Christ unto another gospel: Which is not another; but there be some that trouble you, and would pervert the gospel of Christ. But though we, or an angel from heaven, preach any other gospel unto you than that which we have preached unto you, let him be accursed."   Galatians 1:6-8

We have a clear warning about falling under a curse if we twist the Gospel, which apparently Freemasons do not take into account and skip this harsh warning with the greatest of ease. As a matter of fact, we are going to see a series of contradictions between what they say and what they do. On one hand, they appear to honor the principles of the Bible, but on the other, they do the opposite to what it teaches. In the manual of The Entered Apprentice, or First Degree, there is a desciption of the first Masonic commandment:

"The sacred word of the apprentice has an analogous meaning to the First Commandment: "God is the Eternal, Omnipotent Immutable Wisdom, Supreme Intellligence and Exhaustless Love. Thou shalt adore, revere, and love him! Thou shalt honor him by practicing the virtues!"

Now, if in the initiate's mind, all gods are one and the same, how does the rest of the First Commandment: "You Shall Have No Other Gods Before Me," work in their world? No matter how we look at it, this commandment is impossible for them to obey. Thus, the "wise philosophers" give an explanation and a way out of this conflict by converting

God into a "thought", as the "Apprentice Manual" continues expressing:

"Trust should solely be placed on the conscience and on the inner contact, which is our Father and Lord, and no longer in the false gods of trivial considerations... and of the illusion of the senses".

Does this "super-man" way of thinking (the great god being the human consciousness) sound familiar? Do you think it may have anything to do with the Luciferian mindset spawned in humankind in the Garden of Eden:

"You will not surely die... For God knows that when you eat of it your eyes will be opened, and you will be like God, knowing good and evil."   *Genesis 3:5*

Oh, what a succulent delicacy this has always been for mankind throughout every era! To be like God! Unfortunately, this is nothing more than "The great lie," started when the web of death was woven to blind the eyes of the spirit, so man could never see the one, true God.

This was the initial intention of the seed of evil that has now become the most popular thinking of our time, where Satan infiltrates his most ambitious plans. Regrettably, as gods, men are still unable to resolve the world's problems beyond their own mortal abilities.

Another characteristic of Jehovah, the God of the Bible,

is that He is "Holy", meaning He is "pure", removed from all filth, abominable and foul. He does not mix, nor is He comparable to any other god, nor does he allow His children to do it. He said:

"You shall have no other gods before me. You shall not make for yourself an idol in the form of anything in heaven above or on the earth beneath or in the waters below... for I, the Lord your God, am a jealous God, punishing the children for the sin of the fathers to the third and fourth generation of those who hate me."

Exodus 20:3-5

*"Do not associate with these nations that remain among you; do not **invoke the names of their gods or swear by them.** You must not serve them or bow down to them."*

Joshua 23:7

Jehovah has revealed Himself through the Old Testament prophets in a personal way and always as the only God. The New Testament also speaks to us of God in a personal way through Jesus Christ. He said:

"My sheep know my voice and follow me."   John 10:3

He also made this emphatic assertion so there would be no place for doubt:

*"I am **the** way, **the** truth and the life. No one comes to the Father but by Me."*   John 14:6

Notice that He does not say He is **a** way or **a** truth or **a** way of life, but that He is in Himself **the only absolute truth**.

This weighty declaration is due to the sacrifice, which He made on the cross, by taking the sin of all men upon Himself.   Through this, he opens up the way, which restores the personal relationship between God and humankind. Jehovah always said that without the shedding of blood, there would be no remission of sin (Heb. 9:22).   We see in these examples, a completely different principle from that of the gods formulated in Eastern religions, which are shown as "the great universal mind," or the "Great Architect of the Universe," G∴A∴O∴T∴U∴., as he is designated in Freemasonry.

This god is something abstract, without personality and without a specific name, which cares not about man's guiltiness over sin.   This god can be reached through spiritual exercises, through countless good works and ascetic abstinences, and through continual reincarnations, as they imagine it to be. In this type of Oriental thought, man's soul never dies; instead, upon the passing away of a person, their spirit ascends to the astral world.   In this place, there are different levels the spirit ascends in a continuous chain of purification and reincarnating in other humans. As he passes through different lives, he becomes more and more detached from his passions and earthly affections, turning each time, into a more spiritual being.

In practice, we see that this god, the "Great Architect of the Universe," is less than a god who loves his creation and is more of a symbol, which contains in himself the macrocosmic and microcosmic blueprints. Man then builds himself up, as he understands its principles. In this philosophy, there is no real communication with this superior being that is simply energy or electricity. The utmost its followers aspire, is to join to this cosmic force.

The inherent problem with this philosophy, is that man, besides having his own energy, is a "person" and he is also a "spirit", and as such, needs communication with a personal God. God put this seal inside man, and if this communication is not satisfied, he will always have a spiritual void that reason cannot fill. Furthermore, if the principles we just analyzed were true, we would be living in a better world because of the millions of reincarnations people have been undergoing since antiquity. The sad reality is, the world has never been so lost and so lacking in principles as it is currently. Never has it been so athirst of crime and of the love of money, so far away from altruism and with such eagerness to fuel the ego as it is today.

Let's go back to ecumenical thought. If indeed, all the worldwide religious thinking could be concentrated in one single God, my logic would automatically tell me that this God must, at the very least, have the same characteristics in every religion, even though not everybody would have had the revelation of the same name. But it is absurd to think that the true and only God, who is the absolute truth, reveal himself to the human being in such contradictory forms between one religion and another.

On one end of the spectrum, we have Jehovah, who condemns all forms of religious mixture as His word confirms:

"Do not make a covenant with them or with their gods. Do not let them live in your land, or they will cause you to sin against me, because the worship of their gods will certainly be a snare to you."   Exodus 23:32 and 33

On the other end, in Freemasonry, we have a god named the Great Architect of the Universe, who admits all religions for him to be invoked. In this comparison, one thing is blatantly true through simple logic. Neither Jehovah, nor Jesus Christ nor the Holy Spirit, have anything to do with the "multi-god" or the Great Architect of the Universe.

This brings us to the conclusion that only one God can be the true one and the rest of them are false gods who are trying to occupy the place of the authentic one. Now, if ecumenical thought and Freemasonry were correct and all roads lead to God, then there is not a more absurd and false book than the Bible, which categorically reproves the mixture of religions and accepts no other road to God outside of Jesus Christ. The apostle Paul wrote:

"I do not set aside the grace of God, for if righteousness could be gained through the law, Christ died for nothing!"
Galatians 2:21

The question is: why, or with what hidden reason, is the Bible considered the sacred book of Freemasonry? And if it is so false that one cannot follow everything it says because it is sheer fanatical delusion, why do they make all their oaths above it?

If we examine, in an apologetic sense, the divinity and the veracity of the God of the Bible and His Son Jesus Christ, we would conclude the following: either Jesus Christ was the most insane man, or the dumbest, or the most demon possessed who ever existed, or truly He was the Son of God. If we could come to God through Buddha, who lived upon this earth centuries before Christ, then what need was there for a Messiah to come and suffer in such an inhumane manner as Jesus did for the salvation of humanity?

It would have been simpler for God to tell the prophets to follow the teachings of Buddha and everyone would have been satisfied; or, as is done in Transcendental Meditation, we could repeat "mantras," (power-words which when chanting them repeatedly in the form of a psalmody, communicate the spirit of man to the cosmic energies), to enter into contact with the universal mind.

God, since He began to speak to man, established that He would send a Messiah to redeem the world from sin. The Old Testament talks in full detail about what this Messiah would be like, the only means to enable us to attain redemption and salvation.

C.S. Lewis, who was a professor at Cambridge University and once an agnostic, wrote:

"I am trying here to prevent anyone saying the really foolish thing that people often say about Him: "I am ready to accept Jesus as a great moral teacher, but I don't accept His claim to be God. That is one of the things we must not say. A man who was merely a man and said the sort of things Jesus said would not be a great moral teacher.

He would either be a lunatic- on a level with the man who says he is a poached egg-or else he would be the devil of Hell. You must make your choice, rather this man was, and is the Son of God: or else a madman or something worse."[2]

C.S. Lewis adds:

"You can shut Him up for a fool, you can spit and kill him as a demon;, or you can fall at His feet and call Him Lord and God. But let's not come up with any patronizing nonsense about His being a great human teacher. He has not left that open to us; He did not intend to."[3]

F.J.A. Hort wrote:

"His words were so completely parts and utterances of Himself, That they have no meaning as abstract statements of truth uttered by Him as a Divine oracle or prophet. Take away Himself as the primary (though not ultimate) subject of every statement and they all fall in pieces."[4]

Kenneth Scott Latourette, the great historian of Christianity from Yale University wrote:

"It is not His teachings which make Jesus so remarkable, although they were enough to give Him distinction. It is the combination of His teachings with man himself. They cannot be separated one from the other... "

"It should be obvious for any thoughtful reader of the Gospels records that Jesus regarded Himself and His message as inseparable.. He was a Great Teacher, but He was more. His teachings about the Kingdom of God, about human conduct and about God were important, but they could not be divorced from Him without, from His standpoint being vitiated." [5]

Josh McDowell says in his book Evidence that Demands a Verdict:

"If when Jesus made His claims, knew that He was not God, then He was lying. But, if He were a liar, He was also a hypocrite, since he told others to be honest at any cost, while He himself taught and lived a colossal lie. And furthermore, He was a demon, since He told others to trust in Him for their eternal destiny. If He couldn't back up His claims, and He knew it, then He was extremely evil. Finally, He would have been a fool as well, given His claims of being God were the very ones that led Him to the crucifixion." [6]

The Bible says:

"But Jesus remained silent and gave no answer. Again the high priest asked him, "Are you the Christ, the Son

of the Blessed One?" "I am," said Jesus. "And you will see the Son of Man sitting at the right hand of the Mighty One and coming on the clouds of heaven." The high priest tore his clothes. "Why do we need any more witnesses?" he asked. "You have heard the blasphemy. What do you think?" They all condemned him as worthy of death."

Mark 14:61-64

Josh McDowell adds, "Jesus affirmed to be God. **He left no other option**. His affirmation about being God must be true or false, and is something that must be given serious consideration." He establishes his logic with the following table.

The decision is an individual one. Each person is free to decide what he thinks about this, But the Gospel was not written so that you could extract esoteric truths from its pages apart from Jesus. The apostle John said:

"I write these things to you who believe in the name of the Son of God so that you may know that you have eternal life."   *1 John 5:13*

I offer one last, important point to consider. It is the way God established the ability for man to get into His presence. The Scripture says:

"The High Priest entered the Holy of Holies, or the place of the presence of God and this NOT WITHOUT BLOOD that he offers for himself and for the sins of ignorance of the people."

THE PRINCIPLES OF DEITY

Jesus claims to be God
Two alternatives

His claims were **FALSE**		His claims were **TRUE**
Two alternatives		

He **knew** that His claims were false	He did not **know** that false	HE is the Lord
		Two alternatives

		You can accept	You can reject
He put on a deceitful comedy	He was sincerely deceived		
He was a liar	He was a lunatic		
He was a hypocrite			
He was a demon			
He was a fool since He died for it			

Now, if God does not change, and this blood was the symbol of the atoning sacrifice of Christ, why isn't it mentioned in Freemasonry?, Why isn't Jesus referred to as messiah, or the blood covenant, the altar of sacrifice, or the veil of the temple mentioned? Could it be, as I will expand on later, that the alleged Temple of Solomon, so talked about and studied in Freemasonry, has nothing to do with the Hebrew-Christian God, or with the authentic Temple that God commanded the king to build? Is it also possible that the character of Hiram Abiff, the alleged architect of the temple and symbol of the true Mason, also has no relation to the person mentioned in the Bible?

Notes

1. Shaeffer, Francis: "He is there and He is not silent", pgs. 87, 88.

2. C.S. Lewis Mere Christianity. Macmillan and co. 1952, pgs. 40, 41.

3. 2. C.S. Lewis Mere Christianity. Macmillan and co. 1952, pgs. 40, 41.

4. F.J.A. Hort Way, Truth and Life. New York: Macmillan and co. 1894 pg.207.

5. Latourette, Kenneth Scott. A History of Christianity. New York, Harper & Row 1953.

6. McDowell, Josh. Evidence that demands a Veridict. Thomas Nelson, pgs. 104, 105.

CHAPTER

THE PRINCIPLES OF WHAT IS TRUE AND WHAT IS FALSE

1. The Principle of the Origin of Truth

Identifying the origin of truth is essential to verifying its authenticity. Finding truth depends upon being able to discover and define the sole holder of THE TRUTH. We know that "sole holder" can only be God. Not just any god, but the one and only true God who is Truth Himself. Regardless of how wonderful it may seem to us, no truth can have the remotest possibility of certainty, whether a simple thought lost in the abstract, or birthed from some philosophy, unless we know the veracity of who expresses it.

Truth is apparently one of the foundations of freemasonry as they very firmly state in their laws and principles:

"Truth is a divine attribute, and the foundation of every virtue. To be good and true, is the first lesson we are taught in masonry."[1]

But is it really the truth they pursue? Or, are they just beautiful words to deceive those who enter?

In the principle of a deity, we see that Jehovah, the God of the Bible, (considered to be the central book of Freemasonry) introduces and identifies Himself as Holy, Pure and Jealous, and He does not blend himself with any other god. Furthermore, as we will now see, He also designates Himself as The True One.

"But the Lord is the true God; he is the living God, the eternal King."   *Jeremiah 10:10*

Jesus Christ also says, "I am the Way, the Truth and the Life."

One of the characteristics of truth is that it contains no lie. In the first epistle of the apostle John it says:

"This is the message we have heard from Him and declare to you: God is light; in Him there is no darkness at all"
                                                        1 John 1:5

John goes on to say:

"I do not write to you because you do not know the truth, but because you do know it and because no lie comes from the truth".   *1 John 2:21*

There are those who believe that "the Truth" is found in man-made science. We respect what these people believe, but the book that rests upon the Masonic Ara is not a scientific book, it is the Bible.

"Every well-governed lodge is furnished with the Holy Bible, the Square and the Compass."

"The Bible is dedicated to the service of God, because it is the inestimable gift of god to man."[2]

Once we can define the source of truth, we obtain an important guideline to define what is false. I must strongly emphasize that what is false, is not the visible opposite to truth. Rather, it is a copy resembling truth as much as possible. The essence of which, is a lie and inevitably leads to error.

Let's take a counterfeit twenty dollar bill in US currency as an example. If a person fabricated a bill totally different from the actual currency, it would never deceive anyone. If, on the other hand, they succeeded in stealing the special cotton paper, the inks and the original molds, it would be more difficult to discern it from the true currency. Only by scrutinizing the micro printing, and holding it up to the light to see the watermarks and imbedded security strip, can you truly verify its false nature.

This is precisely, the origin of what is false: Use truth as far as possible to attract those, who more or less, believe they know it. Once their confidence is won over, it is easy to surreptitiously introduce a false concept, which distorts and changes the essence of the message.

As Albert Pike said in the excerpt of the 1966 edition of the Morals and Dogma of the Ancient and Accepted Scottish Rite of Freemasonry, "Freemasonry... hides its mysteries, except to their adept and wise men and uses false symbols to erroneously guide those who deserve to be led mistakenly." (pg.104-5).

If we have already defined the God of the Bible as the true One, as pure, without mixture and without lies, the inevitable question arises: Can the presence of Jehovah, or Jesus Christ and even the Holy Spirit manifest in a place where His word is manipulated and mixed with a blasphemous syncretism of other philosophies? Consequently, if the God of the Bible is not the one presiding over the work of the Lodges, then who is the one being invoked with the name of the Great Architect of the Universe?

What some philosophies define in a vague and abstract form as the forces of evil, the opposite of good, or the opposing side, is stated in the Bible with perfect clarity. The Word of

God does not get lost in ethereal and confusing ramblings; it personifies it with a name of its own: satan.

The time has come to leave behind childish imaginations in which satan is seen as a cartoon character, colored in red and adorned with horns and a tail. The time has also come, once and for all, to discart the absurd concept of the personification of evil as a wicked force having the same magnitude as God. I want to make this perfectly clear: One is the creature, and the other is the Creator. Satan was created by God as the archangel, or the cherubim of WISDOM AND BEAUTY, but because he wanted to be equal to the Most High, God removed him from his position.

The Scriptures mention his fall:

"You were anointed as a guardian cherub, for so I ordained you. You were on the holy mount of God; you walked among the fiery stones. You were blameless in your ways from the day you were created till wickedness was found in you. Through your widespread trade you were filled with violence, and you sinned. So I drove you in disgrace from the mount of God, and I expelled you, O guardian cherub, from among the fiery stones. Your heart became proud on account of your beauty, and you corrupted your wisdom because of your splendor. So I threw you to the earth; I made a spectacle of you before kings. By your many sins and dishonest trade you have desecrated your sanctuaries. So I made a fire come out from you, and it consumed you, and I reduced you to ashes on the ground

in the sight of all who were watching. All the nations who knew you are appalled at you; you have come to a horrible end and will be no more."

Ezekiel 28:14-19

Ever since his fall, satan has continually wanted to take God's place, seeking the worship of men. Maybe for you, beloved reader, this creature called satan, is nothing more than something silly, obsolete or old fashioned. Well, allow me tell you, as a matter of fact, his best disguises are that of being nonexistent or seemingly harmless. Furthermore, the God of the Bible and His Son Jesus Christ, mention him as a real being, and God does not lie, as we have already read in 1 John, "There is no lie in Him". The serious danger stems from satan's ability to manipulate a lie and then present it as true. We must never forget that he is more astute than any man and he will even try to wear the name of the almighty, insofar as he is able, to sidetrack humanity and hinder the worshipping of the only true God, "the Lord of Hosts, and Jesus Christ, God made man."

The apostle Paul talks about this deceit:

*"For if someone comes to you and preaches **a Jesus other than the Jesus we preached**, or if you receive a **different spirit** from the one you received, or a **different gospel** from the one you accepted, you put up with it easily enough... For such men are false apostles, deceitful workmen, masquerading as apostles of Christ. And no wonder, for satan himself masquerades an as*

angel of light. It is not surprising, then, if his servants masquerade as servants of righteousness. Their end will be what their actions deserve."

2 Corinthians 11:4, 13-15

Jesus said:

"He who is not with me is against me, and he who does not gather with me scatters."   *Matthew 12:30*

I've written in bold "a Jesus other than the Jesus we preached", "a different spirit" and "a different gospel" to emphasize just how subtle this counterfeiting is. He even dares to use the name of God. And we can confirm this when in lodges, in Eastern religions and in philosophies of "great apprentices" (as occult sciences have designated them). We see the figure of Jesus Christ appear as an Avatar, as a simple prophet, or as one of the great teachers. But, He is NEVER EVER mentioned as God made man, or as the second person of the Trinity.

Which Jesus is being discussed in these philosophical circles? Without a doubt, they are not talking about the Jesus of the Bible.

Let's analyze this carefully and in detail:

First: He is mentioned as an Avatar. This name is given to those considered to be a reincarnation of Vishnu, (the son figure in the Hindu trilogy.) And, to top off this deception, it is affirmed that this "Jesus" comes to show us the way on how to become one with the Great Universal Mind. The Avatars have made their appearance in every astrological era and in different characters: Zoroaster, Buddha, their defined Jesus, Mohammed, Saint Germaine, and Lord Maitreya in the present.

Second: This Jesus learned his power and doctrine from the Lamas in Kashmir where it is said he spent his youth until the age of thirty, at which time he began his public life. There, he was known as "Prophet Issa," and it was there also, after surviving the lashings, the enormous and inhumane punishment and even the crucifixion itself endured in Jerusalem, he returned to die at a glorious old age.[3]

It does not cease to amaze me how all the avatars talk about reincarnation; about refining themselves from life to life until reaching Nirvana; that God can be reached through self-perfection of the being and of uniting our energy with that of the universe through transcendental meditation. Neither this Pseudo-Jesus nor any of the other avatars mention the existence of evil as a personal adversary, or of death as the consequence of sin.

In contrast to these, the Jesus in the Bible, the Messiah, tells us that He is the resurrection and the redeemer of our sins. He spoke what He heard from His Father in Heaven. He did not preach a universal morality or a philosophy of cosmic knowledge. The Bible says: "He who has the Son has life; he who does not have the Son of God does not have life." (John 5:12). In the Gospel according to Mark, we see how the people of his land remarked on His doctrine and His deeds.

"When the Sabbath came, he began to teach in the synagogue, and many who heard him were amazed. "Where did this man get these things?" they asked. "What's this wisdom that has been given him, that he even does miracles! Isn't this the carpenter? Isn't this Mary's son and the brother of James, Joseph, Judas and Simon? Aren't his sisters here with us?"

Mark 6:2-3

If Jesus really had been learning His doctrine from Buddhist monks, the people would have said something like "Isn't this the one who returned from far away lands where he went to learn this wisdom?" However, what people thought was so odd, was that the local carpenter was able to talk about such things.

There is certainly an abysmal contrast between one Jesus and the other.

Jesus Christ, the true Son of God, was announced by nearly thirty prophets and kings during some four thousand years before His coming. He was born, conceived supernaturally, and died and resurrected, as proof of what He said was true. The rest of the so called "avatars," no matter how enlightened the world may call them, are in the grave. So, when Jesus or Jesus Christ is mentioned in Masonic Lodges, we can be sure that they are not talking about the Son of God, but about the "Avatar Jesus" from the Orient.

Let's see in practice, how a truth is counterfeited to hook those who are led just by hearing the words "God" or "Jesus Christ". Unfortunately, for many people, these names are the only guarantee their consciences require to let a doctrine enter their hearts. Let's take an example from the Masonic Manual.[4]

"The rule, the square, and the compass, are emblematical of the conduct we should pursue in society. To observe punctuality in all our engagements, faithfully and religiously to discharge this important obligation, **which we owe to GOD** and our neighbor; to be upright in all our dealings: to hold the scale of justice in equal poise; to square our action by unerring rule of **GOD's sacred word...**

The misleading continues, as the innocent apprentice hears the word God and feels at peace with it.

"There are three great duties, which, as a Mason, you are charged to inculcate - to GOD, your neighbor, and yourself. **To GOD, in never mentioning his name**, but with that reverential awe which is due from a creature to his CREATOR; to implore his aid in all your laudable undertakings, and to esteem him as the chief good."[5]

We can see this false hook again in this translation from Aldo Lavangini's (Apprentice manual) where it states the following:

"It is then of essential importance that we choose very

carefully what we think and say, as behind every word is the very ***Power of the Word found in the origin of all things: All things were made by him and without him nothing that is would exist.***"

"Uphold good, refuse evil; uphold truth, refuse error; uphold reality, refuse illusion: herein we have in synthesis how the Word should be used. As an example, we give a characteristic assertion meant to be read and repeated individually, intimately and in secret and to the image from which many can be formulated:

There exists only one sole reality and one single power in the universe: God, the beginning, the Reality and the power of Good; Omnipresent and Omnipotent."

"As a consequence, there is nothing to fear but fear itself: since there is no beginning of Evil, which has no reality and no real power, it is simply an illusory image that must be recognized as such for it to disappear. Therefore, Evil cannot have over me or over my life any power whatsoever if I do not acknowledge it or temporarily confer any reality and power to it: it is a false god which positions itself ahead of the true God, Who is quite infinite; an illusory shadow that hinders true Light from shining forth."

Let's analyze this passage from the apprentice's teachings, in light of what the Bible says and through the words of Jesus. I highlighted the words from the Bible which are used as a starting point for this examination and which, as a matter of fact, are the only truth contained within the passages.

1. The text states there is only one power, which is God. The Bible mentions, aside from God, the existence of the prince of darkness, called the devil or satan. Jesus Christ, in the Gospel of John, says:

> *"Why is my language not clear to you? Because you are unable to hear what I say. You belong to your father, the devil, and you want to carry out your father's desire. He was a murderer from the beginning, not holding to the truth, for there is no truth in him. When he lies, he speaks his native language, for he is a liar and the father of lies. Yet because I tell the truth, you do not believe me!"*   *John 8:43-45*

Here we clearly see how Jesus Christ, the **Word of Life**, speaks, without allowing any doubt, about a representative of evil.

2. The text states that evil is powerless over the apprentice due to the simple fact that he does not believe in it nor does he give it any importance. The Bible says:

> *"And you hath he quickened, who were dead in trespasses and sins; ...In which you used to live when you followed the ways of this world and of the ruler of the kingdom of the air, the spirit who is now at work in those **who are disobedient**."*   *Ephesians 2:1-2*

"For our struggle is not against flesh and blood, but against the rulers, against the authorities, against the powers of this dark world and against the spiritual forces of evil in the heavenly realms".   Ephesians 6:12

There are countless Bible verses that talk about satan and his influence over humanity and of his relentless desire to drag men into his infernal dwelling.

What a marvelous disception it is to say that evil does not exist! What better camouflage can satan use than to get people to believe that he is just a tall story! With this dreadful assertion, the apprentice allows himself to be calmly led by the beautiful words, which mention God, and remains defenseless against evil. He then becomes ready for the devil to begin his subtle and treacherous ambush.

2. The Principle of Conditional Truth

God established His Word is the truth, yet it is important to recognize that not all of the Word is absolute truth if we extract it from the context or from the conditions God established it in. We cannot, "remove a text out of context to use it as a pretext," as the well-known phrase states. The Bible holds God's complete mindset made known to man. His personality, the principles of His Righteousness, His redemption and the conditions under which man may be reconciled to Him.

The Bible is not made up of a bunch of verses piled

together so we may adjust them at random to fit our own criteria. Neither, is it a book of magic to which we can apply Kabalistic methods to extrapolate theories which cannot be proven and which are contrary to the general context of the Bible; Theories which are but a sheer illusion in the mind of the philosopher.

To clarify this point, I will make use of the absurd to demonstrate. For example, let's see what it would mean if we take a verse out of context and make it an absolute truth. **Leviticus 17:11** says, "*The life of the flesh is in the blood,*" which is the atonement for sin. If this were an absolute, it would mean that I could give a blood transfusion to a corpse and it would have to rise from the dead since I had endowed it with the ingredient where life is found. It's obvious that such and experiment wouldn't work. Such extrapolations end up being just as absurd and false as the attempt to use the truths that ONLY APPLY TO JESUS CHRIST and then use them nonchalantly as universal philosophical principles. These world thinkers want to use the Bible by removing God from the equation. It doesn't work that way.

As a worthy example, in Lavagnini's Manual, the apprentice thinks that by proclaiming the powerful truths from the Bible, he can apply them to his life without having to comply with any of its conditions. The apprentices have to continually repeat to their inner selves:

"The Divine spirit is within me, Eternal Life, Immortal Perfection, Infinite Peace, Infinite Wisdom, Infinite Power,

Satisfaction of every just desire, Providence and Provider of everything that I need and is manifested in my life: My eyes, open to the light of reality, see Harmony and Goodwill everywhere: the divine principle that expresses itself in every being and in every thing."

In the Scriptures, we find the necessary light to unmask such an assertion. In the first chapter of the Gospel of Saint John, a passage widely used in Freemasonry, we see how God reveals the Word of Life and Light of the Spirit:

"In the beginning was the word, and the Word was with God, and the Word was God. He was with God in the beginning. Through him all things were made; without him nothing was made that has been made. In him was life, and that life was the light of men...

The true light that gives light to every man was coming into the world. He was in the world, and though the world was made through him, the world did not recognize him.

He came to that which was his own, but his own did not receive him. **Yet to all who receive him, to those who believed in his name, he gave the right to become children of God** *- children born not of natural descent, nor of human decision or a husband's will, but born of God. The Word became flesh and lived for a while among us. We have seen his glory, the glory of the one and only Son, who came from the Father, full of grace and truth."*   *John 1:1-4, 9-14*

We see here how this Word of Life, this True light, is Jesus Christ, the Son of God who came in the flesh; God made man. It is not a metaphysical principle from which we can remove Jesus name, apply it to our spiritual life and expect that light to come to us while we obey our own will or whim. We have just read, *"Yet to all who receive him, to those who believed in his name..."* These are the ones who receive this specific Light which makes this truth **conditional**. Therefore, attempting to use it, without its conditioner, who is Jesus, to quicken our spirit, is as absurd as the example of giving blood to a dead man.

We also see in this passage that God differentiates between "sons" and creatures. Not everyone in the world are sons of God. Yes, it is true that we have all been created by Him, which makes us His creatures, But the privilege of becoming a son, with all the rights it implies, is only given to those who receive Jesus Christ through faith. Upon these individuals, the Spirit of God will come, make a covenant and give them life.

I repeat, we have in each one of us the possibility to accept or reject the deity of Jesus Christ. What we can't do is distort what He said, apply it to some Buddhist Jesus and continue attesting that it's the Truth. He, who doesn't want to believe that Jesus Christ is the Son of God, is within his rights to believe that way, but by logic, he must lay the Bible aside in order to look for his philosophy of life in other books.

We must be careful to not be deceived into believing that

which is false, as truth and that which is true, for something obsolete.

3. The Principle of Experiencial Truth

This is the method commonly used in esoteric and metaphysical circles as established by the philosopher Hermes Trismegistus in The Emerald Tablets of Thoth. Here is what it says:

"Truly, the Art of Alchemy has been given without falsehood," (and it says this to convince those who affirm that the Science is deceitful). "Surely, this is experimented, because everything that is experimented is certain. It is true."

This principle, which apparently seems logical in relation to the sciences of this world, such as nano technology, medicine, nuclear science or any other exact science, becomes extremely dangerous when it comes to the spiritual world. Let's keep in mind that the only two spiritual forces, God and satan, with their corresponding spiritual organizations, are presented to men in similar ways. Therefore, the mere fact of spiritually experiencing something beautiful or satisfying does not necessarily mean that it comes from God. For example, the Mind Control method that we find in the "philosophic" degrees of Freemasonry begins by making their students believe that when they reach the mental level known as "Alpha", they can develop incredible power through their minds. The course, which at the onset has a total mental foundation, cannot be completed without invoking spirit-guides to help manage this power. Regarding this, the creator of the mind control method, Jose Silva[6] says:

"The apprentices can choose their own advisors. It can be anyone who is living or dead (referring to a spiritualist invocation); it could be a relative, a friend, or a character from history or from religion... You will do this by going to your favorite place of relaxation and inviting people you desire to be your advisors to meet you there. From then on, any time you want to receive help from your advisors, and in the relaxation place used in your exercises (a place created in your mind) your advisors will be waiting for you."

As we look closely at it, this practice is not only dealing with developing your mind, but it is actually an authentic and very well disguised spiritualist invocation. Unfortunately, many people are not used to discerning the danger in spiritual matters and allow their teachers to lead them in these practices thinking that everything is harmless. For this reason, it's easy for people to believe that their spirit guides are good spirits on behalf of God that help them increase their inner power; as a matter of fact, many of them invoke "Jesus Christ" so the spirit guide occupies this role.

Of course, the real Jesus Christ doesn't manifest His presence in this occult practice.

In my past experiences, I have seen people absolutely obtain this power and develop it with great success. In keeping with the well known phrase, "All that glitters is not gold," we shouldn't stop analyzing the true source of this power.

A) Jesus says:

"Not everyone who says to me, "Lord, Lord," will enter the kingdom of heaven, but only he who does the will of my Father who is in heaven. Many will say to me on that day, "Lord, Lord, did we not prophesy in your name, and in your name drive out demons and perform many miracles?" Then I will tell them plainly, "I never knew you. Away from me, you evildoers!"

Matthew 7:21-23

Here we see clearly that, although the intention of one who does a good deed or a miracle may apparently be good, Jesus doesn't acknowledge it. He is seeking something more than the simple act of a good deed. What Jesus truly seeks are people who commit to Him and live a life in Him and for Him. Jesus is God, Reverent and Holy and He does not take action in order for a student to pass their "Mind Control" course, by showing off their healing powers. Does Jesus still heal today? Yes, but only when a humble and contrite heart appeals to His mercy.

In conclusion, this power of mind control does not come from Jesus and, He is not the one performing the healing miracles.

B) When the Bible talks about help coming from God's

angels, it explicitly says that they are only at the service of those saved by the blood of Jesus Christ.

"To which of the angels did God ever say, "Sit at my right hand until I make your enemies a footstool for your feet"? Are not all angels ministering spirits sent to serve those who will inherit salvation?"   Hebrews 1:13-14

Angels Never, Ever act through invocation, in other words, ENTER a human body. They provide help from outside the body, since entering the body would be totally opposed to God's commandment, as we see in the Law given to Moses:

"A man or woman who is a medium or spiritualist among you must be put to death. You are to stone them; their blood will be on their own heads."
Leviticus 20:27

C) God always respects man's free will. However, one of the characteristics of the satanic personality is to drive, control, dominate, and manipulate the will. This is precisely one of the faculties acquired in mind control. Although the apprentice is recommended to use his power for good, experience shows that human beings, so full of frailties, easily fall into the desire to manipulate somebody's mind in order to reach some selfish objective. This pressure comes after they allow themselves to be inhabited by spiritual entities or demons.

It shouldn't surprise us how statistically, the vast majority of people who graduate from these types of paranormal studies, are affected by great depressions, have marked contrasts in their personality, night terrors, and other similar emotional disorders.

Is this "Mind Control" real? We can affirm that, by applying the hermetic method, yes, it is experiential and we can see a result of power. But, as we have already demonstrated, this power does not come from God. Nor, is it a force perpetuated by the mind.   If it was distinctly a power derived from mental ability, there would be no reason to invoke spiritual beings to increase its effectiveness.   We can conclude that Mind Control is a truly verifiable experience, but it does not come from fountains of "Truth", which is God, and its end, as the wise Solomon said, is "the way of death."

Notes

1 Macoy, Robert: The Masonic Manual Revised Edition 1867.

2. Compiled and arranged by Robert Macoy Revised Edition 1867, pg. 28.

3. Resume from Jesus in Kashmir: The Lost Tomb by Suzanne Olsson.

4. Compiled and arranged by Robert Macoy Revised Edition 1867, pg 28.

5. Compiled and arranged by Robert Macoy Revised Edition 1867, pg 38.

6. Silva, Jose: The Silva Mind Control, Pocket Books. First Pocket Printer. New York.

CHAPTER

THE GREAT BABYLON AND THE FREEMASONRY'S SECRET PLAN

The Bible mentions the term *"the Great Babylon,"* which many theologians have interpreted as the combination of pagan religions, or a mixture of different religious concepts. This name comes from Babel, meaning confusion, and its origin comes from the famous Tower of Babel. This city, besides being a historical fact recorded in the book of Genesis, represents men's efforts to reach God through their own works and means. The Scripture narrates this event, saying:

"Then they said, "Come, let us build ourselves a city, with a

tower that reaches to the heavens, so that we may make a name for ourselves and not be scattered over the face of the whole earth."   *Genesis 11:4*

A tyrant named Nimrod, who ruled the world during that time, built the tower. He was a man of great might and influence among his followers. He was the originator of the Babylonian religion in which he served as a priest. Babylon has been known as the cradle, or mother of all pagan religions. It was famous for its mysteries and its rites filled with symbolism. Furthermore, it is considered to be the nest from where all idolatry arose.

Biblical history narrates how God became so annoyed with the rebellion and the abominations they were committing that he confounded their tongues and dispersed all its inhabitants. Most of the Ancient civilizations were formed from this exodus, carrying as a seal, the philosophical seed of that fallen kingdom. As a confirmation of this theory, some historians attest to Egypt's religious system as having its origin in Asia and particularly, from the primitive empire of Babel.

In his well-known work, Nineveh and Its Ruins[1], Layard declares that we have the joint testimony from profane and sacred history that it's in Babylon, where all idolatry and occult had been birthed. In fact, if all these polytheistic religions, their gods and their ceremonies, are compared with this ancient cradle, we will encounter great similarities.

At Nimrod's death, his people believed that the Emperor would take all his philosophies to the grave; However, his widow Queen Semiramis, further expanded the rise of his religion. She proclaimed him to be a sun god, who had parted to his eternal cycle, but would return once again with more strength. A few months later, the adulterous queen gave birth to an illegitimate son, whom she named Tamuz and presented him to the people, assuring them that this fruit of her womb was Nimrod himself, reincarnated and birthed from an immaculate conception. Semiramis also promoted the worship of the sun and moon. Many of the symbols of this ancient pagan theology are used today in the occult and in the Masonic doctrine.

This is also where the theory of reincarnation comes from, as well as astrology. The magical meaning of the the solstices' dates that we find in the Pre-Colombian cultures of South America , also came from Babylon, and are a key to the big events of Freemasonry. In this same list, we find the Egyptian and Mayan hypothesis of the journeys of the dead.

All these philosophic religions, which came from Babel, are presently coming together to invade the world. This "rebirth" of Babylonian thinking, in its religious esoteric aspect, carries the name of "New Age" and in its external or popular form, it is known as "Ecumenism". The two movements walk parallel to one another with the same goal: a worldwide religious system.

"New Age" carries out its plan by influencing the world

with the decoys of Metaphysics, Cybernetics, Dianetics, Mind Control, Yoga, Transcendental Meditation, Spiritualism, Christian Science, Magic, as well as the rest of the paranormal sciences. Ecumenism tries to unite the world in brotherhood under one same God who has supposedly revealed himself to different cultures in different forms.

This is a chain, which intends to bind the world with these two current offshoots of Babylonian thinking and is the bare minimumal part of a plan, forged many generations ago. A plan destined for the formation of a new world order that perhaps one day, we will see comes to light. Everything is perfectly organized and structured. What is perceived and only among those who know, is barely the tip of the iceberg. Lying underneath, are the blueprints; the secret flow charts of the "Great Architect of the Universe", the powers that are prepared for what they call, "The Great Coup."

Freemasonry has always had the intention to rule the whole world. The Bible calls this religious governmental structure, "the Great Babylon, the great whore who has fornicated with all the kings of the world," which could be interpreted as a series of corrupt alliances between governments and religions that are intimately committed to this secret fraternity.

"Babylon the Great! She has become a home for demons and a haunt for every evil spirit, a haunt for every unclean and detestable bird. For all the nations have drunk the maddening wine of her adulteries. The kings of the earth committed adultery with her, and the merchants of the

earth grew rich from her excessive luxuries."

Revelation 18:2-5

When the Scripture uses the words "Cup" or "Wine," both esoteric symbolism and Bible commentators agree that it refers to spiritual covenants. This speaks to us about the confusion, or the mixture of philosophical and ritualistic concepts found in Freemasonry.

Uniting the world has been one of humanity's greatest ideals or utopias. The mind of man cries from within to see it happen and dreams about the indescribable power of a government that could rule the whole earth. This is what we exposed previously in the thinking of Weishaupt, the creator of the Illuminati, and this is precisely one of the pillars of the Masonic mindset.

Hypothesis of the Perfect Plan

1) They can't avoid the awareness that Man is a spiritual being. Therefore, this need must be satisfied.

2) It's not possible to eliminate the religions that have so divided the people and to squelch each man's spiritual seeking, as the failure of Communism demonstrated.

Thus, the only solution is to label all religious systems as a grouping of obsolete dogmas. Then they must qualify the message of the Bible as fanaticism meant for ignorant people, and turn the Bible into a Kabalistic and symbolic book; This leaves man without any foundation for his existence.

Then, an alternative is presented: a Universal religion, which unites all men, respecting their beliefs under the most ample of tolerance (at least in theory), leading them to peace and worldwide brotherhood; A NEW AGE for the expression of the spirit. A religion which unites us all through the only link that we all have in common: "The Language of Symbols," which each one interprets according to their own reasoning and respects that of others. A religion that has, as its most sublime goal, to make man a god, a self-sufficient one that can attain this level by having reasoning and mind reach their highest potential...

"And you shall be like God, knowing good and evil!"...

This is accomplished by removing all the historical gods that caused nearly every war and erecting the monument, which seduces all minds: "The Superman." The supreme conscience built to become a self-sufficient and perfect being. Man, free from any constraint that prevents him from fully being man. Experiencing, through the philosophy of "The Great Apprentices" or the "Avatars of Universal Knowledge", that man's reason is above the Spirit.

I should emphasize that everything I have just said is perfectly symbolized on the Masonic "Ara," when according to the degree, the square, the compass and the sword are specifically placed upon the Bible, which symbolize spiritual life. This Superman extolled by Zoroaster, Nietzsche and Voltaire, is also talked about in the **Book of Revelation**. It says in Chapter 13:18:

"This calls for wisdom. If anyone has insight, let him calculate the number of the beast, for it is man's number. His number is 666."

Six, according to commonly accepted Biblical symbolism, means man without God; this is the Adamic nature that lost its fellowship with God upon being contaminated with the seed of evil. John Yarker, Grand Master of the Ancient and Primitive Rite, gives an explanation in his book Speculative Freemasonry about this number:

"Hiram's lieutenant deputy, Adonhiram, is named supervisor of this work; six masters assist him in his task, the number six being the symbol of physical man. This number is repeated three times, in the case of the mark of the beast mentioned in Revelation, because three represents the trilogy of perfection, I therefore conclude that 666 is the perfect man in himself; the one who does not need a redeeming God, in other words: the Superman.[2]"

The famous "mark of the beast," symbol of this supreme magnificence of the human ego, could it have anything to do with the Masonic mark symbolically engraved in fire into the heart of every apprentice of the Association?

The Bible contains a passage to reflect on regarding this:

...*"If anyone worships the beast and his image and receives his mark on the forehead or on the hand, he, too, will drink of the wine of God's fury, which has been poured full strength into the cup of his wrath"*

Revelation 14:9-10

Some theologians apply a literal interpretation to these verses, others spiritualize them; regardless of the stance, the majority will agree that this is about a way of thinking, a symbol that opposes the mind of One God.

Satan's utmost faculty is to deceive, and it is not hard to imagine how many millions live already symbolically "sealed" by humanism, by "New Age", by deism and the occult sciences, won over by simple phrases, puffed up in their own reasoning, not taking God into account at all. Beloved reader, if you are a Mason, you will undoubtedly remember that you were told on the day of your initiation to think and not to follow anything you did not understand. My exhortation is for you to do that now and to do it seriously.

During a study I carried out on the different degrees of Freemasonry, what stood out to me, was an event that has a great resemblance to one of the signs of the end times that Jesus announced to His disciples:

"When you see Jerusalem surrounded by armies, you will know that its desolation is near."   *Luke 21:20*

This prophecy was literally fulfilled in the year 70 AD, however, present day Jerusalem symbolizes the "Holy City" for the world's most important religions and it is the symbol that Freemasonry abhors the most: "Religion".

Now, I want you to notice how this event is reinterpreted and indoctrinated in the Constitution and Regulation of the 32nd Degree of the Ancient and Accepted Scottish Rite of Freemasonry[3], which says:

"This degree, the last one in the Scottish Rite, before the supreme degree, holds the Rite's executive power and sums up its doctrine to insure it's functioning. The Masonic assembly of this degree is called the Council, and its insignia represents the formation of a Freemason armada, comprised of Masons from all degrees, to undertake the conquest of Jerusalem and possess its temple and which encamps, awaiting the definitive assault. It is comprised of 15 bodies of armada that will meet in the ports of Naples, Malta, Rhodes, Cyprus and Jaffa, to gather and march on Jerusalem."

"This gathering of the Masonic armada is to be triggered when the signal of a cannon blast is given by the supreme commander..."

"The first cannon blast and the first gathering took place when Luther led the battle against intelligence and form..."

"The fifth concentration will end the reign of the Holy Empire that is to say the kingdom of Reason, Truth and Justice." This is what Freemasonry teaches, while its supporters naively believe the religion they entered with, is respected by the organization with the utmost tolerance.

Here is what the 3'rd oath taken in this degree says:

"I swear to conduct myself as the most bloodthirsty and insatiable enemy of all spiritual tyranny (Religion) that may attempt to impose its conscience on mankind. I swear to stop by any means possible, any Church, Temple, Synagogue or Mosque from opposing freedom of conscience, of subjugating thought and the opinion of its slaves and of expecting or obligating men to believe what they want them to believe."

3) The third part of this perfect plan is to manipulate political powers through an underground organization that has, as its objective, a new world order. As Weishaupt states: "To rule secretly, uniting the most important powers of the world without the necessity for political parties or external opposition."

4) Once this secret organization's projects have been set in motion: invade the people with the propaganda for a New Age, an age of knowledge; an age with no barriers to spiritual and mental experiences, a New Age for the great "Me" within each being, the utopia of a new world of peace and brotherhood where "everything is allowed" in the interest of acquiring the knowledge of life. Conquer their will through music, introduce humanism into their schools and universities, along

with parapsychology, gnosticism and even socialism and atheism, and from the depths, manage the spiritual forces which control these entities.

5) Reveal and establish the ruling power from among the great apprentices of Freemasonry.

This plan is not as preposterous as you might have thought. At least, not according to Serge Raynaud de la Ferriere, the Very Illustrious and Sublime Grand Master of the "Universal Great Brotherhood" and 33rd Degree Great Inspector of Freemasonry,:

"Most of all, you need to know that over our Lodges, our temples, our great east's and our rites, have always existed a Universal Apprentice Direction, a Freemasonry or Great Universal East of esoteric character, whose Sup:. Con:. (Supreme Council) is comprised of real apprentices, who receive direct instruction from their own Esoteric Holy Sanctuaries to transmit it through certain intermediaries to even more esoteric organisms."

"We are sure our B:. M:. (Brother Masons) will be surprised by this, having never heard of such a Superior Direction. Those who know, guard it jealously within their heart to keep their promise. If word ever leaked out, it would create a scandal. May they keep their silence."

"All those who, like us, belong to the Supreme Council of the Great College of Rites, know that recently this Superior

Direction, in light of the distortion of the true Masonic Spirit in our times, has decided to intervene after nearly two centuries of voluntary silence and has released a POWER X to the world with the mission of renewing and reestablishing the Sacred Word that has been vanishing more and more from our temples, giving rise to ignorance and fanaticism."

"Naturally, it is not a question of revealing the name of this POWER, as its name indicates, should remain unknown despite everything, if it means releasing more details about the Sublime Organism that sent it. For the rest, although we might want to, we could not do it; the solemn silence of apprenticeship preserves it from the curiosity of the profane world."

"This World Direction organizes and instructs the different secret associations; its ramifications have always been felt in every country, which has permitted the perpetuation of the Apprentice Tradition for thousands of years."

"... The fact that we are divulging what has been such a jealously guarded secret until today, corresponds to cosmic reasons; we have just entered a new age in which a large part of what has been hidden is going to be revealed."

"The true Grand Masters are not always those who appear vested with great authority; behind the representative powers, titles and functions are the Patriarchs, the Real Venerables, Powers that lead all the Rites of the world at the same time because they are at the head of the Universal Freemasonry."

initiation into the 18th degree of freemasonry

As a member of this organization advances in degrees, he will discover what the true origin is and where the influences come from which control and dominate Masonry.

In the 82nd 30 Mexican International Masonic Convention, at one of the presentations it was said:

"Freemasonry holds such power that we have had great influence even in associations that were born to be our enemies and to disparage us."

Stressing the hidden plan for worldwide government, it continues:

"As it says in the I Ching, (the Chinese book of wisdom): Circumstances are difficult. The task is big and full of responsibility.

This deals with nothing else than to lead the world out of confusion and make it return to order. It is however, a task that promises success as it represents a goal capable of uniting the diverging forces. Could this be a true Masonic meditation? Our obligation is to return to order, and we could not accomplish it if we had not first obtained the internal harmony to which the symbols lead. The work that corresponds to us is the supreme common goal, the sake for which we will apply all our strength united, always putting it before out of our own personal interests. Our task is the incessant struggle for unity and peace."

The Bible mentions something similar in **1 Thessalonians 5:3:**

"While people are saying, "Peace and safety," destruction

will come on them suddenly, as labor pains on a pregnant woman, and they will not escape."

This passage has been interpreted by numerous theologians and historians such as Ireneo and Tertullian, as the message to false prophets, whose success is based on the "peace" and "prosperity" message, rather than the truth.

The Bible never tells us that God has intended to unite all of mankind's cultures and religions. In fact, Jesus speaks to the contrary, saying:

"Do not suppose that I have come to bring peace to the earth. I did not come to bring peace, but a sword. For I have come to turn a man against his father, a daughter against her mother, a daughter-in-law against her mother-in-law – a man's enemies will be the members of his own household. Anyone who loves his father or mother more than me is not worthy of me; anyone who loves his son or daughter more than me is not worthy of me; and anyone who does not take his cross and follow me is not worthy of me..."   *Matthew 10:34-39*

Jesus talks about unity, but under His name, not about uniting all religions. Jesus also talked about establishing the true Kingdom of God, which cost him His life. It also produced a crisis in religious and humanist thought, in paganism and the atheistic minds of multitudes. He made it very clear that establishing the Life of God for the first time in the spirits of believers, would result in conflict with the philosophical thought of the "Gentile" world (the non-Jews) and bring rejection prophesied among His own people.

Jesus was a philanthropist, and He demonstrated this with the parable of the Good Samaritan, which exemplifies His life, but never among His teachings can you find Him agreeing with the thinking of other religions, and distorting His Father's pure doctrine. He healed and helped everyone, without expecting their gratitude. His great love for mankind led Him to the cross, so that anyone who accepted this sacrifice, would have access to eternal life.

Who then, is truly seeking this global unification, to prove that the Jesus of the Bible was wrong and that man can achieve universal unity all by himself?

At the International Congress of Spiritual Strength in Paris, May 25, 1949, the Grand Master, Serge R. de la Ferriere, began his speech by saying:

"G:.T:.T:.G:.A:.O:.T:.U:. (GLORY TO THE GREAT ARCHITECT OF THE UNIVERSE)...

"We are going to allow ourselves to make a clarification in these times of anxiety and in this place where the spiritual future of the world is going to get weaker."

"Freemasonry is a philanthropic, philosophic institution... that has as its objective the exercise of goodwill, the study of "Universal Morality", the analysis of science and the practice of all the Virtues." "The Great public generally feels a certain difficulty when dealing with the esoteric, the occult or initiation and through "Masonry" immediately catch a glimpse of an unspeakable magic, because the people, blinded by fanaticism, immediately involve secret association with Freemasonry."

"What difference does it make how we honor the Great Architect of the Universe?... Our first and greatest virtue is 'Tolerance'."

Now, if **Jesus Christ's** thinking is radically opposed to S.R. de la Ferriere, where does this "Universal Morality" come from that he strives so hard to attain? Is the tolerance they purvey even real, Or is it simply a phrase used to make the follower let his guard down as far as his religious beliefs are concerned? Could it be a lure of safety, which makes it be possible to instill in him their doctrine of the apprentice? As the Master Aldo Lavagnini says in The Aprentice Manual, referring to the new convert, "He must stop from passively accepting false beliefs and outside opinions, with the objective of opening his own path to the Truth."

One of the greatest proponents of Universal Freemasonry, Manly Hall, Grand Sovereign Inspector General, explains in his book, The Lost Keys of Freemasonry (pg. 48), the force that moves through every Mason and every New Age apprentice:

"When the Mason learns that the key of the warrior of the room is the correct application of the dynamo power of life, he has learned the mystery of his trade. The boiling energies of Lucifer are in his hands."

In his instructions for the twenty-three World Supreme Councils, Albert Pike wrote the following shocking, Masonic truth:

To You, The Sovereign General of the Grand Inspectors, we say this: to repeat to the 32nd, 31st and 30th degree Brothers that the Masonic religion must remain for us all, the apprentices at the highest degrees, in the purity of Luciferian doctrine... **Yes, Lucifer is God, and unfortunately Adonai is also God.... Lucifer, God of light and God of good, fights for humanity against Adonai, the God of Darkness and evil**. (Adonai is one of Jehovah's names in the Bible.)

In these next chapters, I will show you how all of these passages that have been transcribed and stated are true, and that the real force which moves behind the science of the apprentice and of Freemasonry, is none other than satan.

Notes

1. Llayard, A.H: Nineveh and Its Remains. London: John Murray, 1849.
2. Yarker, John: Speculative Freemasonry. London, 1883.
3. Pike, Albert: Morals and Dogma of the Ancient and Accepted Scottish Rite Freemasonry. City: Kessinger Publishing, LLC.2002.

CHAPTER

THE TEMPLE OF SOLOMON AND THE MASONIC LODGE

To ascertain the origin and the true foundation of Masonic lodges, it is important to go back to its obscure birth.

The organization has been established since the 17'th century with the guild of cathedral builders. Its esoteric aspect however, dates back to the beginning of history, where the origin of its symbolism can be found, along with its religious mysticism.

These two occult roots form the foundation of present-day Masonic thought. With this in mind, rather than thinking of its history as an established order, the Masonic mindset is primarily a peculiar type of mystical reasoning, occult or secret, which arose from almost all of the civilizations and acquired its form during the Middle Ages.

The Master, Aldo Lavagnini[1], reinforces these origins by saying:

"Aside from the external or formal aspect of religion, all ancient people knew about the sacred practices, an inner, parallel teaching or "esoteric", that was solely given to those who were reputed moral and spiritually worthy to receive them. This aspect of religion was especially given out by the so-called "Mysteries". This means: mute or secret, and is characterized by the obligation to keep this learning secret through an oath required from the apprentice".

"Some Mysteries were instituted among all known peoples during the pre-Christian era history, in Egypt, India, Persia, Chaldea, Syria, Greece and in all the Mediterranean nations, the Druids, the Goths, the Scribes and Scandinavian peoples, China and the native peoples of America. Their traces can be tracked from the odd ceremonies and customs of the tribes of Africa and Australia. Particularly famous were the mysteries of Isis and Osiris in Egypt (gods of the moon and son, respectively); the ones of Orpheus and Dionysus, and the Eleusinian mysteries of Greece and those of Mitra all the way from Persia, were spread all over by the Roman legions throughout the countries of the Empire".

"Likewise, Brahmanism, as well as Islam and some practices Catholicism acquired, are undoubtedly previous to the establishment of said religions".

Egyptology is vital to the Masonic apprentice ideology given several of the mysteries of magic come from this ancient civilization.

The Derkeiler Group published the following article in June of 2009[2]:

"The Egyptian mysteries make up one of the remote foundations of the Royal Art of Freemasonry. Many of the conceptual, ritualistic and symbolic elements of the Order of Acacia reveal their bond to this grandiose civilization of the Nile, and their elevated solar spirituality."

The most prominent representation is the sphinx, symbol of secrecy and as such, the essence of Freemasonry esoterism. Next in prominence is the figure of the triangle, which carries great importance in Masonic symbolism and among other things, is the schematic representation of the Egyptian pyramid, the image of the human spirit which projects upwards with its highest apex touching the light of the sun, a representation of divine light, the light of truth.

I need to add that the "perfecting of the masterpiece," the Mason must work for, is represented by the "cubic rock" crowned by the "pyramid shaped stone."

The Egyptian pyramids were built 4,000 years ago to give glory to their gods. These were temples in which complex rites of birth and death based on the afterlife were carried out.

Many of the rituals utilized in the Masonic Lodge have their origin in the Egyptian civilization, specifically in the worship of the figures of Isis, Osiris and Horus.

Another Masonic symbol with Egyptian roots is the All-seeing Eye, frequently depicted inside a triangle. This eye, symbol of divine providence and also of "the eye of knowledge" or the "mind's eye", opens through initiation. It appears in the stelae of ancient Egypt, associated with the god Horus, who is the incarnation of the light's creative and victorious power and whose vision, disciplines all evil-doing and reintegrates the dispersed limbs of the dead.

Right: The Egyptian eye of Horus.

Below: Dollar Bill. The "All seeing Eye" is observed with the pyramid on the background, symbols of power and control.

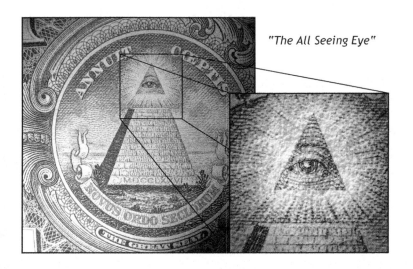

"The All Seeing Eye"

The figure of Isis the Egyptian goddess, who occupied the central place in the mysterious cults of ancient Egypt, is of major importance within Masonic spirituality.

Isis is the divine Mother, who after the death of her husband, the god Osiris, incessantly seeks to bring his mortal remains back to life. She is the Widow alluded to in the "Sons of the Widow", a title Masons call themselves. The untiring search of Isis is the model that every good Mason must imitate in his incessant search for the lost word. Isis herself, is considered the incarnation of that lost word, which, as Christian Jacq says, is at the same time mother and widow:

"always mother since she gives birth to new initiates, and always widow because she remains eternally one and she will never ever be stopped by a man."

Albert Mackey[3] in his Lexicon of Freemasonry, states that Egypt was the cradle of geometry and of the regal art of construction. This ends up being the same as saying that it is the cradle of Freemasonry in its double aspects of speculative and operative. According to Mackey it is from Egypt, where the sciences and the mysteries of the ancient pagan world are derived. Egyptian wisdom resting upon that fusion of geometry and operative masonry, made it possible for the grandiose constructions such as the pyramids and the Egyptian temples; this fusion of science and art would subsequently continue in the Masonic tradition."

Left Isis: she is attributed with the title "Sons for the Widow", the same one used in Masonic Lodge

Bottom Left: Isis Egyptian goddess of magic, sister of Osiris and Seth, mother of Horus.
Bottom right: Worship of mother and child; 150 years before Christ. This is where the Queen of Heaven would derive from.

In reference to this, Master Aldo Lavagnini adds:

"Freemasonry, in its search for universal knowledge, has attributed its essential foundation to all religions and secret rites. However, it is the spirit of Religion that has been weaving this mysterious wisdom throughout the centuries. Myths, legends, and every kind of ceremony make the sum total of what constitutes the hidden truth, and its basic proposition is within this logic, that no religion is false, instead all are true."

As we have already seen, this is totally opposite to the God of the Bible, who doesn't mix with any other god and emphatically opposes the use of symbolism in an esoteric fashion as well as the worship of gods represented by heavenly bodies and images.

"Therefore watch yourselves very carefully, so that you do not become corrupt and make for yourselves an idol, an image of any shape, whether formed like a man or a woman, or like any animal on earth or any bird that flies in the air, or like any creature that moves along the ground or any fish in the water below. And when you look up to the sky and see the sun, the moon and the stars - all the heavenly array - do not be enticed into bowing down to them and worshiping things that the Lord your God has apportioned to all the nations under heaven."

Deuteronomy 4:15-19

We see in the Scriptures that all Egyptian, Babylonian and pagan imagery is forbidden by Jehovah God warning us of the corruption of our souls. Here is a closer examination of God's biblical rejection of occult symbols and religious images:

"They abandoned the temple of the Lord, the God of their father, and worshiped carved Asherah poles (symbols) and idols."   *2 Chronicles 24:18*

"By this, then, will Jacob's guilt be atoned for, and this will be the full fruitage of the removal of his sin: when he makes all the altar stones to be like chalk stones crushed to pieces, no Asherah poles (symbols) or incense altars will be left standing."   *Isaiah 27:9*

After reading these Scriptures, we see the mindset of God regarding symbols and alien gods. These instances are referring specifically to those who have their religious foundation on the sun god and on the moon goddess, whose worship can be seen in the majority of the ancient civilizations.

It is important to realize the dramatic contrasts between the occultist's sentiment and that of the God of the Bible. You will see that Masonic symbolism, such as is present in the "Mysteries," will continually sift out Biblical portions in an attempt to demonstrate that Jehovah, as well as Jesus Christ and the Holy Spirit, participate and approve of their occult philosophy. However, they will never mention verses like the ones you have just read, and the Old Testament is full of them.

The easiest thing for them to do would be to erase the God of the Bible. Not having Him would remove an enormous weight off their shoulders due to all of the contradictions He poses to their theories. However, to banish the figure of The God of the Hebraic scriptures from their rituals, would bring in great confusion among the followers of the occult sciences. It would immediately raise suspicions as to the credibility of the Order and would alienate a multitude of gullible people. Obviously, something that would be self defeating. Their cleverness lies precisely in the opposite: extract the Biblical verses out of their original context and give them an analogous symbolism that agrees with the rest of religions.

We in fact, do find similarities in some symbols, but I want to remind you that what is false will always try to resemble which is true, as closely as possible, although in essence, they are opposites.

The names of Jehovah and of Jesus Christ, His Only Son, are so powerful that regardless of how hard they try, they cannot eliminate them. In order to dodge this bullet, they transform Them, change Theirnames and combine Their principles with the most hideous, infernal, occult ideology.

Inevitably, the very holiness that makes the God of the Bible unique; gets in their way. They can't stand the sovereignty of Jehovah, the Father, and the crushing truths of His Son, yet it is impossible to do away with them because everything He created bears His seal and everything is sustained by the right hand of His power.

Oh, what a delusional dream Lucifer has insofar as thinking God's name will never be mentioned again! Nonetheless, the verses from the Bible seem to emanate in all their coarseness as a shining light amidst deep darkness at the time when the initiated sincerely seeks truth. They appear to jump and blow up against all initiate's knowledge, shouting at the apprentice as well as to the teacher that there is something wrong, that there is something from within the Order that does not agree with the purity of God.

And then, unfortunately, it ends up being more comfortable for the confused soul to close the Bible and run to the false security of the occult knowledge: covering the ears of his conscience, resting from the incessant resounding of God's words that echo in his innermost being, clamoring out:

Masonic syncretism using the Tetragamaton "YHWH" the four letters of the name of Jehovah in Hebrew.

"THE TESTIMONY OF JEHOVAH IS FAITHFUL" (Psalms 19:7) or as the wise Solomon would say, "The fear of Jehovah God is the beginning of wisdom." (Proverbs 1:7)

What Freemasonry seeks is Jehovah's power, but removing Him from its midst. This is the reason we will see the Biblical symbols appear time and again in the Masonic Lodge, non of which, have any relation to the God of the Bible.

It is common among the first degrees of Freemasonry for the followers to think the lodge is a symbolic representation of the famous Temple God ordered Solomon to build. Both Jews and Evangelicals involved in the Order feel strengthened in their religious beliefs when they see these symbols. They are also instructed, its architect is Hiram Abiff, whom the Hebrew king charged with this sublime mission. This character is therefore, a legend in Freemasonry and is likewise a symbol of the spiritual builder of the Temple.

The Bible cites Hiram Abiff , as one of the goldsmiths, helping out in all the necessary smelting for the Temple. On the porch of the temple there were two large columns named "Jachin" and "Boaz." The replicas of these columns are in every lodge. Despite these Hebraic symbols, their true representation is that of the Egyptian god Amon-Ra.

In his work The Black Book of Freemasonry, the Very Illustrious and Grand Master Mason Serge R. de la Ferriere says, referring to Hiram Abiff:

"Many Brother Masons firmly believe that he is a somewhat historic character, when he is simply a symbol. They are fooling themselves. After the spiritual workers were initiated in order to build the temple of Truth, Hiram was killed many times, but raised from the dead. Hiram is Adonis, killed by a wild boar; he is the exiled Pythagoras; he is Osiris, killed in a typhoon; he is Orpheus, torn apart by drunkards; he is Jesus, crucified by Caiaphas, Judas Iscariot and Pilot; he is Jacques (Santiago from Molay), condemned by the Pope, betrayed by a false brother and burned by order of the king. Naturally, this is only one explanation among many others. If you note that Hiram is related to fire (Let's not forget that he was the blacksmith, working metal with fire), then the allegory of his death would correspond to the regeneration or transmutation of this same element. He is the Chief of all true Masons worldwide."

In a certain way, Hiram is the Spirit of Occultism. He is the grand master architect of the secret temple, hidden in deep darkness. He is the inspirer of the temple of Osiris in Egypt and of all the other magic temples of the world. He is the spiritual power that has been unveiling the symbols and repeating them throughout generations. He is the one who has been trapping mankind in the confusion of his enchantments and his spells of knowledge and virtue. It is the spirit of Lucifer, in his insatiable struggle to occupy the throne of the Almighty. Master de la Ferriere continues, saying:

"The true Grand Masters are not always those who appear clothed in authority; behind the representative power of titles and functions are the Patriarchs, the true Venerables, the Powers who lead the rites of the world because they are over the Universal Freemasonry."

In the Hebrew-Christian Scriptures, the only spiritual army that is described in this manner is the one led by the prince of the power of the air, Lucifer.

"For our struggle is not against flesh and blood, but against the rulers, against the authorities, against the powers of this dark world and against the spiritual forces of evil in the heavenly realms."   Ephesians 6:12

The true God did not want His Kingdom of Heaven to be a secret. Jesus said:

"You are my friends if you do what I command. I no longer call you servants, because a servant does not know his master's business. Instead, I have called you friends, for everything that I learned from my Father I have made known to you."   John 15:14-15

Jesus' teaching is simple and, at the same time, incredibly profound when someone gives his (her) life to Him. I am not referring to hypocritical fanaticism, but to the surrendering of the heart, to a quality decision of making Him the Lord of our life.

The Kingdom of God is structured very differently. God does not need a series of powers to illuminate the believer. Whoever He receives as His son, He seats him directly in heavenly places next to Jesus Christ.

"(God) made us alive with Christ even when we were dead in transgressions - it is by grace you have been saved. And God raised us up with Christ and seated us with him in the heavenly realms in Christ Jesus."
                    Ephesians 2:5-6

Nowhere in the Bible do we find that God has formed armies and spiritual powers to lead rites in the temples of the world. That is why Jesus said:

"I will tear down this temple and will I rebuild it in three days."

He said this meaning He would never again dwell in manmade temples, but instead in the heart of those who surrender to Him. His death and resurrection opened the way for this to happen.

"Jesus replied, "If anyone loves me, he will obey my teaching. My Father will love him, and we will come to him and make our home with him."   *John 14:23*

The apostle Paul talks about this to the first believers in Corinth:

"Don't you know that your body is the temple of the Holy Spirit?"

Now, if Jesus came to tear down this ritualistic structure to make for himself, a Church that was a living body made up of the true believers, what interest would He have in going back to the old structure of the temple?

Solomon's temple, as described in the Bible, was not a place to worship just any god, instead it was specifically for (Jahova) God to dwell in the midst of His people, Israel. It was not perceived as a place in which other nations worshipped, and whosoever would, could venerate their own god in the most ample tolerance, or that it was a place with symbols adopted from other civilizations. God spoke clearly to Solomon, saying:

> *"As for this temple you are building, if you follow **my decrees**, carry out **my regulations** and keep all **my commands** and obey them, I will fulfill through you the promise I gave to David your father.*
> *And I will dwell among the children of Israel, and will not forsake my people Israel."*   *1 Kings 6:12-13*

Here we see how God places conditions for His presence to manifest in the Temple. God did not dwell there because there was a magic symbolism in its construction or in its furnishings. God dwelt there because Solomon was obedient and complied with the order from God. These same prerequisites are the ones He requires now, for Him to dwell in the temple made of flesh, mankind.

Another condition that God specified was that the Temple be built exclusively for His name to be worshipped, "My name shall be there" (1 Kings 8:29) and not some abstract name with which any pagan god could identify himself.

Let's examine the stark differences between the temple of Solomon in the Bible and the false temple in a Masonic Lodge.

"Now the first covenant had regulations for worship

and also an earthly sanctuary. A tabernacle was set up. In its first room were the lamp stand, the table and the consecrated bread; this was called the Holy Place. Behind the second curtain was a room called the Most Holy Place, which had the golden altar of incense and the gold-covered ark of the covenant...

When everything had been arranged like this, the priests entered regularly into the outer room to carry on their ministry. But only the high priest entered the inner room, and that only once a year, and never without blood, which he offered for himself and for the sins the people had committed in ignorance. The Holy Spirit was showing by this that the way into the Most Holy Place had not yet been disclosed as long as the first tabernacle was still standing...

When Christ came as high priest of the good things that are already here, he went through the greater and more perfect tabernacle that is not man-made, that is to say, not a part of this creation. He did not enter by means of the blood of goats and calves; but he entered the Most Holy Place once for all by his own blood, having obtained eternal redemption... In fact, the law requires that nearly everything be cleansed with blood, and without the shedding of blood there is no forgiveness. It was necessary, then, for the copies of the heavenly things to be purified with these sacrifices, but the heavenly things themselves with better sacrifices than these. For Christ did not enter a man-made sanctuary that was only a copy *of the true one; he entered heaven itself, now to appear for us in God presence. Nor did he enter heaven to offer himself again and again, the way the high priest enters the Most Holy Place every year with blood that is not his own.*

*Then **Christ would have had to suffer many times since the creation of the world**. But now he had appeared once for all at the end of the ages to do away with sin by the sacrifice of himself. Just as **man is destined to die once, and after that to face judgment**, so Christ was sacrificed once to take away the sins of many people; and he will appear a second time, not to bear sin, but to bring salvation to those who are waiting for him."*

Hebrews 9:1-4, 6-8, 11-12, 22-28

As we have just read, the Scriptures highlight some points of radical importance regarding the purpose of the former temple.

We see for example, that its main objective was for the priests to intercede for the sins of the people. Although the general populous could not enter directly, God did not consider them to be profane, instead, He extended His mercy to them.

We also read that Christ did not incarnate many times as stipulated by de la Ferriere when he talked about the different apparitions of Hiram Abiff, amongst which, with incredible impudence, he included Jesus Christ. The original temple was the truthful dwelling place of God before Christ.

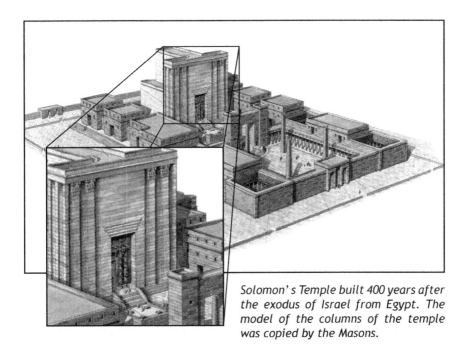

Solomon's Temple built 400 years after the exodus of Israel from Egypt. The model of the columns of the temple was copied by the Masons.

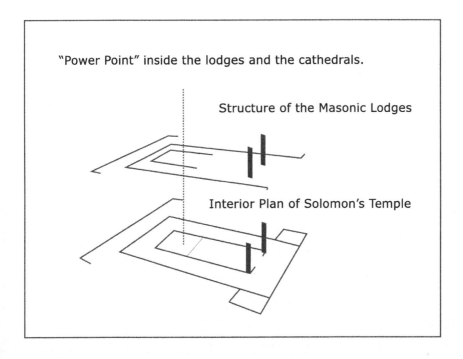

"Power Point" inside the lodges and the cathedrals.

Structure of the Masonic Lodges

Interior Plan of Solomon's Temple

It was not an astral place where the dead went.

"...Man is destined to die once, and after that to face judgment".   *Hebrews 1:27*

I consider this last scripture extremely important as reincarnation is one of the most used philosophies of esoteric circles, including those of the Masons. (See Appendix at the end of the book.)

The Masonic lodge is physically different from the ancient Hebrew temple. The word Lodge means Universe and it is arranged in an analogous way to the sidereal, (relating to stars and constellations), space. Its form is rectangular, and is characterized by two bronze columns named "Jachin" and "Boaz", which are generally found three steps away from the entrance door. Each column is crowned by clusters of pomegranates and a sphere, one with a terrestrial globe and the other with the blueprint of the universe. Between them, is the Ara or the altar, upon which rests the Bible and the Masonic symbols of the compass and the square, known as the three "Great Lights of Freemasonry". Around the altar, forming a triangle, are three candelabra with a wax candle on each one, called the "Three Lesser Lights".

They are an allegory of the Sun, the Moon and the Master, (who numerous writers have claimed is Hiram Abiff, first Master of Masonic immortality). The floor where the Ara is located is covered with white and black tiles, arranged like a chessboard, which symbolizes the duality of life. Hanging from the ceiling, directly above the altar, is the flaming star and a triangle containing the square, the compass and the letter G in the center. This symbolizes the Great Geometrist, or the "Great Arcana", builder of the universe. Along the walls are chairs that correspond, according to the cardinal points of the compass in which they are located, to the different degrees of knowledge. The ceiling is painted blue, where in some cases; the signs of the zodiac are drawn. All around the crown molding there is a chain made of rope links that symbolize the unity of the Masons around the world.

In the main room, there is a door that leads to the meditation room, painted in black with drawings of skulls, bones, and skeletons, lit by a sepulchral lamp. There is also a black table with a glass of water, another with salt, a piece of black bread and writing paper. There is a casket in the back of the room with a skeleton inside. This is the sarcophagus where the aspiring Mason enters for the ritual of the third degree.

In a Lodge there are various individuals assuming character roles. The most important is the Venerable Master, which represents the Sun; the Orator, Mercury; the Secretary, Venus; the Treasurer, Mars; the Master of Ceremonies, the Moon.

The one occupying this last appointment is seen always walking around simulating an orbit inside the Lodge with a staff in his hand.

The design of a Masonic Hall.

Internal Structure of the Masonic Lodge. The two columns at the entrance, the blue ceiling, are observed among other details.

It is possible to find Masonic symbols in some of the Catholic churches around the world.

We also see other important posts, such as the Watchmen, which represent Uranus and Neptune, and the First Expert, Saturn; Freemasonry's highest degrees represent the nebulas. As we can see, the temple of Solomon is very different from the one created by the Masons. The question we're left with is: Where did their model come from?

Here is an explanation from the Venerable 33'rd Degree Master C.W. Leadbeater:

"When in my real life they initiated me into Freemasonry, I was joyfully surprised when I saw the Lodge for the first time. It seemed familiar to me. Its layout was identical to what I had seen in the Egyptian mysteries of six thousand years prior... The symbols are significant and characteristic within a peculiar combination. And, nevertheless, all of it belonged to ancient Egypt where I had become fully familiar.

"Almost every ceremony remains unchanged. There are only minor differences of little significance. I began to seek in the physical plane, proof that would corroborate these facts from my own personal experience in the books that fell into my hands, and there were more than I had hoped for...

A few interesting illustrations have been taken from the mural paintings of ancient Egypt and from vignettes from numerous papyruses and mainly from the Book of the Dead, of which there are various revised editions."

"It becomes evident from these facts that in Egypt the

temple was built in a double cube form, in whose center were found three cubes on top of each other in the layout of an altar upon which the books of Sacred Scripture were placed; of course, not the same ones as the Christian ones, as they had not yet been written."

Top: Papyrus from the "Book of the Dead" that describes rituals similar to the ones used in Freemasonry.

Below: The square is a common symbol used in Freemasonry. It is the addition of two triangles, typical symbology of the Egyptian civilization.

"The cubes represent three aspects or persons of the trinity: Osiris, Isis and Horus, as the signs carved into them indicate..."

"At the entrance of the temple are two columns and upon them were pictures that represent the earth and heaven. One column is named "In Strength" and the name of the other one means "To Establish". This portico symbolizes the path leading to the superior world of Amenta (a kind of heaven) where the soul fuses with the immortal spirit and remains this way forever. Therefore, the portico was the symbol of stability. At the entrance of the Lodge, there were always two guards, armed with knives. The outer guardian was called Watchman and the inner guard was called Herald."

"The majority of the clothing was removed from the Neophyte... and he was led to the door of the temple, where he was asked who he was. He responded that he was "Shu", the "supplicant who arrived blind in search of light".

We see the true meaning and purpose of the Lodge as Leadbeater's description continues:

"The two columns symbolize the duality of all that is manifested and they remind us of our permanent obligation to gather opposition and to find equilibrium between the living and the dead and between construction and destruction. It is here that we are reminded of that "second birth" that is described in virtual form and that we must bring about during the course of our career.

The two columns are located at the entrance to the lodge hall.

It is between the two columns where we greet the three lights of our workman, and we symbolically express that we are willing to die rather than betray our supreme ideals.

When we see the lights upon the Ara (altar), they evoke the essence, substance and form of the trinity; of the spirit, soul and body. The book is there, (the Bible), the square and the compass. The Sacred book of the law, living symbol of tradition, that first teaches us to read and finally to write in the Book of Life; the square that shows us earth and matter and our righteousness; the compass that puts us in contact with heaven and with the spirit and shows us the possibility of the unlimited from immortality to eternity."

"The Ara (altar) is the center of our temple and evokes in

us the center of our being and the heart of mankind; the thinking heart where the subtle force of pure intellect resides."

The original columns of Solomon's temple, Jachin ,"he will establish" and Boaz "swiftly," as their names mean, when correctly translated from the Hebrew, referred to Yahweh. As we have just read in the previous text, these columns in the lodge, represent dualism and have nothing to do with the principles of the God of the Bible. Lavagnini reinforces this by saying:

"Metaphysically, they represent the masculine and feminine aspects of divinity, the heavenly Father and Mother, the gods and goddesses that are found in practically every religion."

To include God in this dualism is such a false theory that it falls apart all by itself. A dualistic mind seeks the all-encompassing God that conforms with the universe.

God is the Creator, the Everlasting, the Almighty. What can compare to Him for this "divine" dualism to exist?

It would be utterly childish to think that satan, who is only a fallen creature, albeit having great cleverness and presumptuousness, could be equal with the Eternal God. It's like comparing a fly to the ocean and thinking they are conflicting equals. Attempting to find an equilibrium between life, which is God, and Death, which is represented by Lucifer, ends up being as illogic and foolish as the previous example. Nonetheless, people believe that they can live in this gray zone between good and evil, on an impossible and absurd equilibrium, without any consequence and believing God is there.

I want you to notice the contradiction that exists with dualism in a verse taken from The Kybalion, one of the most important books of Hermetic philosophy:

"Everything is double; everything has two poles; everything is a pair of opposites; those similar and their antagonists are the same; the opposites are identical in nature, but different in grade; truths touch each other; all truths are half-truths; all paradoxes can be reconciled."

What this explanation on dualism means, is that God and satan are equal and that the holy nature of the Almighty is equal to the malevolent nature of fallen satan. God is not God absolute and His Truth is just a half-truth and finally that God and satan are reconciled. The only one who could, with such pride and arrogance, inspire such a foolish thought in Hermes Trismegistus, is lucifer himself.

Returning to the analysis of the Lodge, in a similar manner to the Egyptian initiate, or "supplicant" approaching the temple, the aspirant in Freemasonry also has to confess that he is profane, is subject to darkness and in a total state of blindness and he has come to receive the "light" of Freemasonry. In this ceremony, the Venerable Master says to the approaching profane:

An aspirant to Masonry, blindfolded in the ceremony of initiation.

Every new apprentice must acknowledge that he is arriving in darkness and that he will only receive light through Freemasonry, thus denying his original faith.

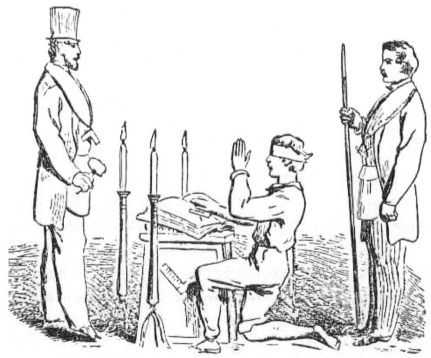

"The man of the world is profane, surrounded by vices, passions, seeking his fortune everywhere and finding it nowhere. He wants to know why he feels so blind, only making out darkness and shadows. His evil nature makes him an instrument of discord and misfortune."

Further into this same liturgy of initiation, the Venerable says to the aspirant, "Do you want to leave this state, join our association, and offer your heart and your arm to he who instructs you?". As was done in the Egyptian ceremony, the initiate must then enter the lodge in a state of semi-nakedness.

Every new apprentice must acknowledge that he is arriving in darkness and that he will only receive light through Freemasonry, thus denying his original faith.

The concept of the Lodge, as it was in ancient Egypt, is a sacred place in an Eden-like state, far from the profane; a place equal to where the dead go, and in which, the spirit is evolving from an astral state to a higher one.

Logically, this nullifies the whole Christ-centered foundation that tells us that life is given to us once, to die and afterwards comes judgment.

"And shall come forth; they that have done good, (will rise) unto the resurrection of life; and they that have done evil, unto the resurrection of damnation.

John 5:29

Any person who expects to walk the path of Christ, who confesses before Freemasonry that he is arriving in a state of darkness, has denied the light of Christ as the only true light of the world. He now yields to the way of the Great Architect of the Universe (whose true identity we have been demonstrating throughout this book).

Jesus said:

"No servant can serve two masters. Either he will hate the one and love the other, or he will be devoted to the one and despise the other."   Luke 16:13

One cannot belong to Christ and be a Freemason. As we have seen, the purposes of the real Temple of Solomon and that of the Masonic Lodge, are radically different.

Let's now continue with Leadbeater's narration of how he supposedly lived six thousand years ago in ancient Egypt:

"According to 'The Book of the Dead', if the neophyte violated his oath, his throat would be slit and his heart would be cut out. The papyrus of Nesi Amsu mentioned another degree in which "the body was to be cut to pieces and reduced to ashes and then cast to the four winds upon the surface of the waters."

"In the temple of Khnumu, on the island of Elephantine, in front of Aswan, there is an engraving with two figures: the Pharaoh and a priest with the head of Thoth, in the vigorous activity suggestive of an initiation..."

"The flaming star shone in the Lodge, but it had eight points instead of six or five. It was called the "Dawn Star" or "Morning Star" and it was the symbol of Horus' resurrection (Figure of the son in the Egyptian trinity). The Masonic square was very well known and it was called neka. It is found in many temples and even in the Great Pyramid. It is said that it served to square off stones and also symbolically to square off conduct, the same as the modern interpretation. To build with a square represents the ways of ancient Egypt's teachings. In the Egyptian hall of justice, Osiris is seen seated upon a square as he judges the dead. Thus the square came to symbolize the foundation of eternal law."

"The Book of the Dead", is part of a manual destined to serve as a guide in the ASTRAL WORLD, with various instructions regarding how the deceased and the initiates were to behave in the lower regions of the other world... Apparently the Egyptian minds acted quite formal and orderly since they tabulated every conceivable entity the deceased could run into and they carefully laid out the spell or power word to defeat hostile entities; but without realizing that their own will accomplished the work, they attributed their success to some kind of magic.

In the beginning, 'The Book of the Dead' was kept secret, but subsequently, some of its chapters were copied in papyrus, to place them in the tomb of the deceased. One of its passages says:

During the period of the New Empire, it became a tradition to deposit in the sarcophagus of the deceased "The Book of the Dead". (a collection of magic formulas to help overcome the dangers the deceased had to face in their trip to the world of Osiris). The belief in reincarnation used in New Age and in Freemasonry is birthed from this type of ritual.

The duality of the initiate in the Egyptian rituals can be observed in this depiction. Observe how his body has shadows that allude to the search for the life in the hereafter.

"This book is the supreme mystery. May no one pass it before their eyes, because it would be an abomination. It is called The Book of the Keeper of the Secret House."

Likewise, Leadbeater asserts the same in his book The Hidden Life in Freemasonry, when he describes the work of the Order:

"The work is the preparation for death and for what follows. The two columns "Joaquin" and "Boaz" were raised at the entrance of the other world and the diverse tests the neophyte endures, symbolize those that could come upon him when he leaves the physical world to go to the next stage of life (pg. 227).

As we have already seen in the Bible, Leviticus 20:27 says:

"A man or woman who is a medium or spiritualist among you must be put to death.... their blood will be on their own heads."

Later we will see the interaction of spirits of the dead and of demons during these initiations. The Apprentice, without an awareness or knowledge of this invisible world, receives its rituals as something symbolic and with no transcendence. All he knows is that he needs to go through this sinister initiation to become a Mason.

He will also encounter the same threat that was used in Egypt to punish those who betrayed its secrets in the ceremony of the first degree Mason. In it, the Venerable Master tells the petitioner:

"You say you see nothing and that you felt a tip upon your chest. It was a sword! God deliver you from it ever piercing your chest!

"This was the punishment that was applied and should be imposed upon those who sold themselves to tyrants, but for us, the Free Masons, it is a symbol of what has happened to you and of what you must endure. **It represents the eternal twister that will destroy your soul**, if you let down this August Institution you are asking to join."[4]

Nothing that comes from a holy and benevolent God could ever have any resemblance to this clause. Only a mind, hungry for power and control, can enslave its members in this manner. They are bound to the consequences of something, the majority don't have the slightest idea of what they're getting themselves into.

Jesus said:

"I have come that they may have life, and have it in abundance."   *John 10:10*

The Bible also says:

"Since the children have flesh and blood, he too shared in their humanity so that by his death he might destroy him who holds the power of death - that is, the devil - and free those who all their lives were held in slavery by their fear of death."   *Hebrews 2:14-15*

Going back to the Egyptian description of the Lodges according to Leadbeater, I want to clarify that when we see the term "resurrection" in the initiates' writings, it does not refer to the Christian teaching of resurrection from the dead, since they believe in the opposite: reincarnation. When this term is used, it is referring to deities or cosmic masters which never die, but who become incarnate in different bodies.

We saw this example when examining the spirit behind Hiram Abiff, and the resurrection of Horus, the "Morning Star". We also clearly see the theory of reincarnation in the following description by Leadbeater's, of his purported experience in Egypt during a previous life:

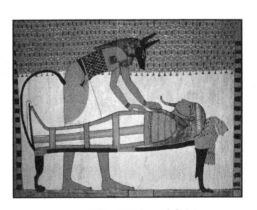

Resurrection of Osiris

"When Osiris was dying (God of the Sun), Isis and Nephis tried in vain to resuscitate him, but Anubis succeeded in his attempt. Osiris returned to the world of secrets of Amenta, which seems to suggest that Masonic secrets are closely related to the underworld and the ultra-earthly life.

"Such are some of the most conclusive proofs that I have been able to gather and there are others that cannot be published. It appears to me that even more proofs are to be found; but even the ones given, when considered together, make the possibility of it being a coincidence vanish. There is no doubt that the brotherhood that we have the honor of belonging to today is the same one I knew more than six thousand years ago and which dates back even further."

I believe no doubt remains on how the origin of the Lodges is not based on the Temple of Solomon, built for Jehovah, the Judeo-Christian God.   Nor, are the symbols used inspired by Him.   Rather, this is the temple raised to Osiris, whose altars Jehovah commanded to be torn down together with the symbols of Asherah. Although some symbols were absolutely copied from the Solomon Temple, their meaning is based on the rituals of ancient Egypt and on the powers governing them.

Today, the symbols of these Egyptian temples and the designs of the occult, are embedded in thousands of cities, buildings and monuments.

Freemasonry has been invading our society, so that its hidden principles, gods and demons can move among us, remaining imperceptible to those unfamiliar with the principles of the Order, its plans and designs.   They will continue to be active and grow until the day, those who truly hold the power of the Almighty God, invalidate, denounce and eradicate them.

Some of the most renowned buildings around the world with Masonic architecture.

Masonic Door at the entrance into Madrid, Spain.

Chinese Television Building.

Financial Center in Kuala Lumpur, Malaysia.

Notes

1. *Translation from Aldo Lavagnini: Manual of the Apprentice. (Spanish Original Title: El Manuel del Aprendiz)*

2. *http://newsgroups.derkeiler.com/Archive/Soc/soc.culture. argentina/2009-07/msg00352.html.*

3. *Mackey, Albert: Lexicon of Freemasonry. Kessinger Publishing LLC. 1994.*

4. *Liturgy of the degree of Apprentice of the Memphis Masonic Manual, pg. 33.*

CHAPTER

MASONIC SYMBOLISM

The Bible, Masonry's sacred book states:

"If you ever forget the Lord your God and follow other gods and worship and bow down to them, I testify against you today that you will surely be destroyed. Like the nations the Lord destroyed before you, so you will be destroyed for not obeying the Lord your God."

Deuteronomy 8:19-20

1) The principle of Symbolism

Symbolism plays an extremely important role in Hermetic philosophy, (which is the hidden knowledge revealed by Hermes Trismegistus also called The Thrice Greatest Mercury), as well as in the Hebrew-Christian scriptures.

A symbol not only represents a spiritual knowledge, but it's also related to a spiritual entity. It's not something fake that we can evoke without any consequence, but it is rather a vehicle to connect the natural world to the spiritual one. Let's see how this spiritual effect is manifested in Freemasonry.

At one of the lectures of the "International Masonic Conference Mexico 82" it was said:

"We want to emphasize in particular, the subject of the first three degrees said to be symbolic or of Saint John, and draw attention to the transcendental importance of symbolism that comprises the very foundation of our institution. The symbol is not an end in itself, but the representation of an idea or a force, hidden behind it. It is the instrument ideas manifest, and at the same time the most appropriate vehicle, that if handled properly, will lead us directly to the entity hidden behind it... The symbol acts within the conscience of those who are open to it and Masons should be guided by those mysterious signs."

For those who simultaneously belong to Christian religions and to Freemasonry and think that symbols are irrelevant, I want to mention the baptism into the Christian faith as a real-life example.

"Or don't you know that all of us who were baptized into Christ Jesus were baptized into his death? We were therefore buried with him through baptism into death in order that, just as Christ was raised from the dead through the glory of the Father, we too may live a new life… For we know that our old self was crucified with him so that the body of sin might be rendered powerless, that we should no longer be slaves to sin - because anyone who has died has been freed from sin."

Romans 6:3-4 and 6-7

In the Christian faith, this is not merely a symbol without spiritual consequence. Father God destroys the power of sin over the believer through this symbolic act. From this moment on, God considers him or her, justified before His eyes, even though only symbols were used in the ceremony.

When the power of the blood of Jesus is invoked during Communion to cleanse us from sin, even though it is only being mentioned in a symbolic form, the soul is purified and the conscience ceases from having the weight of remorse. If the Christian who has enlisted in the ranks of Freemasonry thinks that the symbols are merely allegoric, then what value does he give to the ones I just mentioned? If these truly have power, so do the others.

God, as well as satan, use symbols to release their power.

In the Bible, we can count a large number of symbols that activated the heavenly realms. For example, the oil that was used to anoint a king or a prophet, symbolized the Spirit of God was coming upon that person. The symbol was and is, the point of contact to loose the power of God, or in the opposing case with satan, the power of the spiritual entity represented by that symbol.

We can also exemplify the purification rituals the high priest had to fulfill during Old Testament times to enter the "Holy of Holies", which was the place in the Temple where the presence of God physically manifested. If these rites didn't have a real cleansing power over the soul and spirit of the High Priest, he would have died the same instant he stood before the Ark of the Covenant. Symbology is therefore, a door to the spiritual world.

It's important to understand, when we talk about the spiritual world, there are only two terrains we can penetrate. The first is that of the true God. This can only be entered through the narrow gate: Jesus Christ and under the conditions He established. He said:

> *"Enter through the narrow gate. For wide is the gate and broad is the road that leads to destruction, and many enter through it. But small is the gate and narrow the road that leads to life, and only a few find it."*
>
> *Matthew 7:13-14*

The second terrain is that of Lucifer, who tries by any

means possible (read as: names, religions, philosophies, spirits or visions) to attract humanity to his "BEAUTIFUL LIGHT". Although he presents his light as beautiful, full of power and goodness, it is just a counterfeit of the true one.

Let's now look at the utilization of these symbols in Freemasonry and without the need for lengthy explanations, even the least learned can realize the implications.

In the initiation of a first degree Mason, the initiate must go on a tour blind-folded undertaking three different symbolic trips. During the tour, he passes through the representation of the different planes of hell. It is the interpretation of the Egyptian myth of the journey of the dead. The corrupt soul (as they call it) crosses into the astral world from an inferior plane to a higher one until finding the supposed, true light.

Once the ceremony has been symbolically laid out, the initiate thinks this is something harmless and nothing more than an adventure, although a terrifying one as we will later see. Let's see what happens in this spiritual arena where the beginner is totally unaware. C.W. Leadbeater, 33 degree Mason, describes part of this ritual:

"As the candidate approaches the seat of honor of the Second Watchman, he arrives at the second portal, where they introduce him to the elements (spirits) of earth and water that belong to the region where he has just symbolically arrived, represented by the solid and liquid sub-planes of the astral world. First, the candidate turns towards the north and makes the appropriate offering to the elements of the earth and then turns to the south to do the same with those of the water. These entities were not involved in the construction of the temple; but they are under their Boss, who obeys the "Second Watchman" as guard of the second portal.

These elements, that are kinds of nature spirits, circle the candidate, recognizing him from then on. After this ceremony, if the candidate appears to be in any physical or threatened danger by some antagonistic force, he can bring a guard from these entities to defend him, due to the allegiance that has been established."

As we can see, this is not just a simple test of bravery to be accepted into the Order, but there is a deep involvement with spirits whom, without knowing it, the Apprentice has already entered into a covenant. Who are these spirits and what has the innocent beginner allied himself with?

In polytheistic cultures, these same essential spirits are represented by the gods of the sun, moon, earth, etc. If we had to define these deities, they would be spirits having specific characteristics to help those invoking them, performing different favors and miracles on their behalf. However, whom do they serve and who is the boss backing them up? Jehovah, the God of the Bible, speaks specifically referring to these kinds of spirits and to those who turn to them for aide and making offerings unto them:

"They made him jealous with their foreign gods and

angered him with their detestable idols. They sacrificed to demons, which are not God - gods they had not known."
                                       Deuteronomy 32:16-17

Here we see that God directly calls these spirits, demons and what appears to be a seemingly symbolic ceremony without any spiritual consequence, is the doorway wherein satan has begun to weave a web that many are no longer able to escape.

The Bible confirms this by the radical forbiddance from seeking any type of help from spirits:

"Let no one be found among you who sacrifices his son or daughter in the fire, who practices divination or sorcery, interprets omens, engages in witchcraft, or casts spells, or who is a medium or spiritist or who consults the dead. Anyone who does these things is detestable to the Lord..."
                                       Deuteronomy 18:10-12

All these practices are linked to the alleged "helping spirits". The Masters of esoteric Knowledge turn to these spirits to be filled with "The Strength of the Universe" and draw from them their spiritual power.

Let's look at a clear example in which the same symbol has opposite meanings. In the Bible, Jesus Christ is referred to as "the chief cornerstone".

"... See, I lay a stone in Zion, a chosen and precious

cornerstone, and the one who trusts in him will never be put to shame."   *1 Peter 2:6*

Within the lodges, this term symbolizes all of the Hermetic thinking about the philosophical rock and is represented by a crude, unhewn rock. "One same symbol represents two opposing characters: it is either Hermes or it's Jesus Christ."

This rock, before which the Mason must bow down during his initiation of the second degree, has an engraved inscription that says "Jah-Bul-On", which symbolizes a trinity of the gods: Jehovah, Baal and Osiris, who are invoked in higher degrees. The manner of invocation is through the repetition in the form of a psalmody of each syllable of this name in the form of a "mantra", as it is done in yoga, to summon the presence of the Great Architect of the Universe. I repeat again, that Jehovah, the God of the Bible, does not mix with any other god, nor does he acknowledge any other god as part of his court.

Now, let's briefly look at the meaning of this rock, so flaunted by Masons. In the Bibliotheque des Philosophes Chimiques, the French alchemist, Hortelano, in his explanation of The Emerald Tablet by Hermes, shows us with clarity, this interrelation with the spiritual world.

Hermes, the great philosopher of ancient Egypt, attributed all universal wisdom to this rock. The rock was the symbol of the entire cosmos; it was also the beginning and end of all things. Everything that man is and his relationship with the universe is also symbolized by it. Let's now see what Hortelano says, referring to this philosophical stone:

"The underside of the rock is the earth, which is the midwife, the ferment, and the upper side is heaven, which brings the stone to life and resuscitates it..."

And explains:

"The human body is the recipient that picks up the emissions of the celestial discharges undoubtedly alluding to the revitalizing "Celestial Dew" that symbolizes the descent of spiritual energies into the bosom of man."

The body of the initiate then begins to become a recipient of all kinds of spirits. Hortelano continues explaining this experience by saying:

"In the alchemic iconography it is common to represent the inert body of the alchemist, lying in a tomb or on the ground, symbolizing the death of the initiate, who comes to life (resuscitates) thanks to the 'drops of rain' that descend upon him."

It is known in the occult or initiate circles that it is through this transference of spiritis into the inner part of the apprentice through which he is born into the spiritual realms. This ritual is observed in the initiation of the third degree of Freemasonry, although its spiritual consequences are not explained to the initiate. Only in the higher degrees is its spiritual implications made clear. This ceremony, which apparently is nothing more than a symbol, is the rite Masons use to join their "spiritual light" which is truly the false luciferian glow.

ACTIVATING THE POWER OF SYMBOLS

The Pentagram or Five-Pointed Star

I had previously mentioned the danger of symbology in that a meaning is not universal, given the same symbol may be interpreted in different ways according to different criteria. For example, we have the five-pointed star or pentagram, the quintessential symbol used in satanism and in the upper level magic circles. It is known within these arenas that the pentagram, also known as "the evil goat", attracts the presence of lucifer and is one of the most powerful forms of demonic invocations that exists. This same symbol, with its true meaning only given to Masons of higher degrees, during the Apprentice stage however, is defined and utilized as the symbol of human perfection.

What do you think is at work behind simple appearances and what the hidden motive is of utilizing the same symbol that bears two conflicting meanings? To shed more light, I want to show you an extract from the book, The Hidden Life in Freemasonry by Leadbeater:

"However, for us the star has symbolic meaning. The star reminds us of the initiation that is a sign the LORD OF THE WORLD agrees with and approves the entrance of a new candidate in the powerful, eternal brotherhood." Well, let's see who this Lord of the World is according to the Bible. Jesus Christ tells His disciples:

*I will not speak with you much longer, for the **prince of this world** is coming. He has no hold on me"... that is, the devil.*   *John 14:30*

Let's analyze another part of Leadbeater's book. But before we do, keep in mind the differences we have established between the God of the Bible and the impersonal energy of the Great Architect of the Universe, GAOTU. Scrutinize the way in which the name of the Tibetan avatar is used, the one they call "Jesus," who differs from the Jesus of the Bible. The pentagram is used as a form of invocation for the spirit of Lucifer, disguised as the "false Christ". The author writes:

"Some years ago, our noble brother Sir S. Subramania Iyer, of Madras, told me I should investigate a mantra (power word used to enter into the spiritual world by means of its continual repetition) that the eminent occultist of southern India, Swami T. Subba Rao, had purported to have used for a long time.

I carefully examined the matter and also used the mantra later, because in effect it was notably real. According to what I found out, this mantra is found in the Upanishad Gopala-tapani and in Krishna, and is made up of five parts. Deliberately meditating upon the mantra, results in every syllable plotting a line in such a way that a star of five points is drawn (like the pentagram). Upon repeating the mantra, the stars superimpose upon one another until forming a tube whose transversal section is the five-pointed star. The tube serves as a conductor channel of the energy of Shir Krishna, who is the very being of Lord Maitreya, the actual bodisatva or instructor of the world, the sublime being that fuses as Christ in the body of Jesus. Due to the energy embodied in this mantra, it can be used for different purposes, such as to heal the sick, separate elements and other benefits."

I believe it is now quite clear the pentagram is not an innocuous symbol that shines over the Lodge, but rather a true spiritual conduit used to make contact with the prince of darkness. How can I say this with such confidence? Because of what the Bible says in this regard (theoretically, the divine Light of Freemasonry). I want to emphasize this point so you, dear reader, may become totally convinced and clearly identify this enormous deception coming from the angel of light, known as Lucifer. Let's look at what Jesus himself says about this alleged Christ-like spirit that inhabits Lord Maitreya and other enlightened ones such as Sai-Baba. Jesus, speaking about the latter times affirms:

At that time if anyone says to you, "Look, here is the Christ!" or "There he is!" do not believe it... For as the lightning comes from the east and flashes to the west, so will be the coming of the Son of Man.

Matthew 24:23 and 27

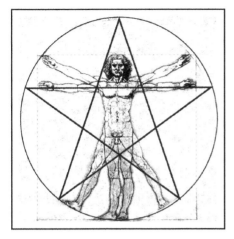

| Superman | The evil goat |

Left: The Superman is the symbol of perfection for the human being, obviating any connection to the Creator, God. Right, The five pointed star is a Masonic symbol which verifies the relationship between this organization and satan. (Illustration taken from the book Hermetic Symbolism, by Oswald Wirth {pg.93})

If Jesus Christ were truly this lofty being incarnate in Lord Maitreya, Jesus would have never spoken the words we just read in Matthew.

Here is another example of who this god is that shows up through the invocation of the pentagram. The ambiguous becomes the obvious. Let's go to Leadbeater's book again for his explanation of the ceremonies in the temple of Amon-Ra, the supreme Egyptian deity also known as Osiris:

"As soon as the Venerable Master uncovered the glasses, he raised his arms toward the flaming star, and exclaimed:

'Oh, lord, descend.'"

"... The clear liquid in the cup turned an intense pink shade. The change in color symbolized the descent of the divine life and once the change was complete... he then said,

- 'The lord has surrendered himself to us. Give thanks to the lord.'" Then everyone bowed before him, saying together, 'You are Osiris.'"

As we have already seen through numerous examples, it is neither Jehovah, nor Jesus Christ, nor the Holy Spirit, that descends through this invocation, but rather, the Egyptian sun god. To this regard the Bible says:

"Woe to the obstinate children," declares the Lord, "to those who carry out plans that are not mine, forming an alliance, but not by my Spirit, heaping sin upon sin; who go down to Egypt without consulting me; who look for help to Pharaoh's protection, to Egypt's shade for refuge. But Pharaoh's protection will be to your shame, Egypt's shade will bring you disgrace."

Isaiah 30:1-3

No matter how many interpretations they may try to give to the pentagram, it is an unequivocal symbol of Luciferian power and its essence and force behind it, will still be the same. Turned upside down, the star is the evil goat or satan as he appears in the cover of the satanic bible, and on the emblem of the "Order of the Eastern Star", in the Third Degree of the Rite of York. Turned right side up it symbolizes the superman in his fullness. It symbolizes the one who has reached such a degree of evolution that he no longer needs a redeemer. The achievement of this superman is satan's masterpiece and he directs all his undertakings into forming this character that is the mark of his followers.

The Hexagram or Six-Pointed Star

Most people identify this symbol with Israel and call it the Star of David. Both Jews and many Christians feel proud of it and wear it as hanging pendants, display it in their church logos and also in the decoration of their temples and homes.

Is it really a symbol designed by the Hebrew king, as common belief dictates, or is it a symbol that actually curses Israel?

The correct name for this star among the Jews is the "Seal of Solomon". Its origin comes from a religion called Bon Po that deals with the occult and the magic aspect of Buddhism. Its composition of two converging triangles represents the duality that we see in all oriental philosophies. The triangle that points downward symbolizes the divine forces that descend. The one pointing upward represents the infernal forces that ascend and unite to the heavenly ones, to conform the "great wisdom of man". It's an analogous symbol to the Yin-Yang which intends to unite all things into one, both good and evil.

An American dollar with the hexagram where the word M A S O N is read.

Masonic pentagram and hexagram found at Castleton Church, Derbyshire England.

Symbols hexagram and yin yang

This symbol came to Israel by way of wise men and travelers from the orient. The oldest hexagram in Israel was found carved in a frieze in the synagogue of Capernaum, and oddly enough it is carved next to a pentagram.

Throughout the entire frieze, there are grotesque figures of demons, making it clear that this symbol was not made by instruction from the God of Israel.

The hexagram was adopted by the pagan occultists who were living in Israel during the time of King Solomon, who used it to render a graphic symbolism of the great wisdom of the king. From that point on, Jewish Cabbalists discovered its great esoteric power and began using it.

"Kabbala" is the occult and mystic branch of Judaism. The highest-level satanists have conferred it the reputation of being the most powerful magic in the world.

Frieze in the Synagogue of Capernaum, Israel. This is the world's oldest hexagram.

Amongst them, the hexagram has always been used as a symbol for the invocation of spirits from the utmost levels.

The triangle is one of satan's most used symbols. Geometrically speaking, the triangle is the transversal division of a square.

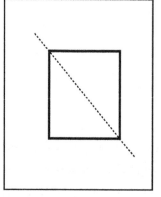

The God of the Bible, who is meticulous and exact in all of His designs, never uses the triangular form. In all the plans of the Tabernacle and of the Temple, we always see the shapes of the square and of the rectangle. The triangle represents that which comes against the design of God causing it to split.

Since the Middle Ages, one of the highest-ranking members of the "Illuminati" has been the Rothschild Family. They,

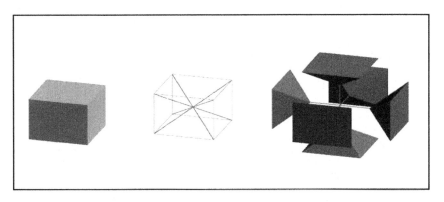

Cube Design.
The division of the cube, it forms 6 pyramids of equal size.

being Jewish and highly Cabbalistic, put the hexagram in their coat of arms, and their subjects were forced to use it to honor their lord.

Before World War II, the Jewish people did not identify themselves with this symbol. It was Hitler who imposed it upon them as a way to stigmatize them. Hitler was a high level satanist, trained in the Bon-Po religion, as his biographers have relayed.

It was from the far east that he brought the symbols of the swastika and the hexagram. He knew that it was a symbol that heretically declared the union of God with Satan and he marked them with it in contempt and as an insult to the Jewish faith.

The Six Pointed Star
The hexagram represented the number of the beast, 666.

After the war, the Jewish people adopted the hexagram, not to symbolize King David, but to represent their imprisonment and death during the holocoust. Israel decided to always remember its pain and the infamy carried out against them.

In 1947, driven by the Rothschild family, the Jews chose the hexagram as the national emblem for their flag. By one single vote, this design won over the menorah (candlestick) with two olive trees. They said, "Through this symbol, we want the world to know our deep pain."

The hexagram is a symbol that ties Israel to death, to prison, to bitterness and to pain. Through this star, Israel is perpetuating the plan of death and genocide that satan designed for them through Hitler.

Both for Cabbalists as well as for Hitler, the hexagram represented the number of the beast, 666. The Six Pointed Star, by Dr. O.J. Graham, states:

The supreme evil nature contained in the double triangle called the "Seal of Solomon" or "Magen David" (Shield of David) is proven with the fact that the number of the beast, 666, is contained within it. Note that there are six triangles incorporated in the outer part of the star, there are six points and six lines that make up the two triangles.

The Bible speaks of this star as being abominable to God:

But ye have borne the tabernacle of your Moloch and Chiun your images, the star of your god, which ye made to yourselves. Amos 5:26

You have lifted up the shrine of Moloch and the star of your god Rephan, the idols you made to worship. Therefore I will send you into exile beyond Babylon. Acts 7:43

This clearly is not a symbol of blessing or a means to lovingly identify with the Jewish people. To perpetuate it is harming Israel as well as those who wear it or use it.

Why Does Satan Uses Symbols of Righteousness and Divine Attributes?

The Masonic symbols are many and they constitute their hidden language. They are inter-woven in diverse art forms, stained-glass windows, tapestries, furniture, entire buildings, floors and ceilings, In monuments, in the flags, in the heraldry and currency designs of many nations. Freemasonry has been leaving its traces, marking territories, establishing ruling spirits. They are undeniable seals that establish luciferian doctrine everywhere.

Upon studying the principle of what is false and what is true, we saw that which is false, most closely resembles that which is true, without it being so. If satan only used his terror, murder and thievery to attract his followers, very few people would enlist in his ranks, but just as any good deceiver would, he disguises himself.

He is the father of every lie and from the onset of his fall; he has made man believe that he can be like god. However, the concept of god in the human mind, is someone good, righteous, elevated, celestial, perfect, of good manners and good intentions.

The question is: Can satan reproduce something like this? Is the devil really interested in good, love, wisdom and in the well-being of mankind? Or as the Word of God says, referring to the devil:

"The thief comes only to steal and kill and destroy..."
John 10:10

If he is not seeking anything good, why does he use symbols that imply beneficial things to the shallow observer?

Considering he is a thief, a murderer and a destroyer, his strategy is to subdue the good concept the symbol represents and cursing it under his covenants and his demons, so it never ever manifests.

Allow me to ellaborate on this. Let's take an example from the better known Masonic symbols:

The square, compass and the "G". The first represents righteousness; the second, creative strength and calculating intelligence; the "G", the Great Architect of the Universe.

Under this symbol, the Devil, or Great Architect of the Universe, is able to rob man of his righteousness and of his creative power and limits him to a calculating mind that is dominated by the influence of demonic spirits.

Other examples are the symbols and words used by Masons who designed most flags and shields around the world.

We see here the symbols of the circle inside the square with the phrase "Order and Progress".

What do you think the Devil wants to control in Brazil? Order and progress. The

Flag of Brazil

result: tremendous opposition in these two areas.

The circle and the square are the most frequently used symbols in Freemasonry and another way of representing the builder's square (drawing the square) and the compass (tracing the circle).

We see in the euro this same composition called among the Masons "the squaring of the circle."

German Euro   Italian Euro

Masonic Symbols We see Inter-woven In All Their Designs

Let's analyze the meanings Masons give to symbols, so we can decipher what they have cursed through a covenant with the devil, so we can undo it in the power of Jesus Christ.

Anchor

Anchor: Symbol of Hope. Through it the devil brings fear and hopelessness.

Book: Symbol of wisdom. Establishes human wisdom above divine wisdom.

Caduceus

Caduceus: The messenger's staff. An attribute of Hermes; Freemasonry employs it as one of the symbols of science and progress. It destroys health and blocks progress.

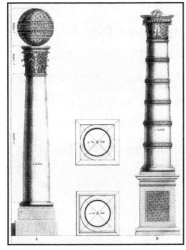

Column

Column: Symbol of the union between heaven and earth, of firmness and sustaining strength. The complete column, with base and capital, is related to the symbol contained in the tree of life.

Decorating the columns: refers to the act of the workshop attendants taking up their respective positions in their tasks or Masonic meetings.

When the Watchmen ask the workers to sit down in their seats of honor that are on both sides of the Lodge, they say, "The brothers that decorate the column of the North". These columns unite the earth with the spiritual regions of satanic government, also known as the "second heaven".

Room decorated with Masonic symbolism. Columns, three lights and the mystical lasso are seen.

Compass

Compass: Creative force and calculating intellectual activity. Creates a prison, traps within the circle.

Cup, Chalice: Frequent symbol of robust abundance. Brings poverty.

Cup

Crown: Ennobling symbol. Emblem of majesty, power, martyrdom, glory and triumph, figure of Masonic rites. Establishes the powers of darkness in government.

Crown

Dolphin: Emblem of velocity. Brings tripping and obstacles.

Diana: Luminous and perfect. Establishes the feminine figure of Satan.

Diana

Dionysus: Bacchus, the vine. Brings alcoholism.

Eagle

Eagle: Power and freedom. Emblematic figure in all degrees of Freemasonry known by the name of "Philosopher or High Degrees", symbol of audacity, investigation and genius. Through this symbol the devil brings corruption, abuse of power and promotes a form of liberty that for God, is abomination.

Gavel

Gavel (Mallet): Name that is given to the hammer that is the symbol of authority and belongs to the Venerable and the two Watchmen, who by means of the sound of the gavel direct the work of the brothers. Corrupts Authority.

Globe of the earth

Globe of the earth: Emblem of regularity and wisdom. Produces earthly ties to prevent celestial wisdom from being seen.

Hermes

Hermes: Agility, speed and activity. Brings obstacles and stops the flow of God's blessings.

Lion: Emblem of Hermetic art.

Mandala

Mandala: Has as its objective to contribute through meditation, the union with the divine. Brings union between the occult of Satan to earth.

Mystical Lasso (Rope): Masons consider themselves to be united to each other by a sacred and unassailable bond of fraternal character. That is why they call themselves the "Brothers of the Mystical Lasso ". Depicted around all the lodges is a painted or sculpted chain, as the symbol of the unity of all Masons extending around the globe. It brings the bondage of darkness and death.

Owl

Owl: Hidden wisdom. Brings the presence of occult spirits.

Pomegranates: United fraternity. A fruit that does not rot. The symbolic explanation of this teaching is that inside Freemasonry there may be a bad seed.

Rose

Rose: Symbol of discretion, innocence and virtue. Also the symbol of union. Brings perversion and division.

Ruler: Emblem of perfection. Brings iniquity and lies.

Square: Symbol of Masonic righteousness. Brings iniquity and lies.

Square

Sword

Sphinx: Emblem of the Masonic works, which must be secret and hidden.

Sprig of wheat: Birth and death. Controls births and the manners of dying.

Star: Perfection. It is the seal that establishes the legality of demonic designs.

Sword: Honor, conscience and protection "steel". Establishes the hosts of Satan.

Torch

Torch: Fire, purification and illumination. Brings corruption and mental captivity.

Wheel: Progress. Slows progress and brings chaos.

Wheel

Kabbalistic Codes

Masons also utilize words or letters to create Kabbalistic codes. They intersperse them every determinate number of letters to form a geometric figure in a document, with a sub message only they are able to detect.

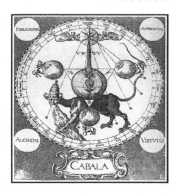

Right: Kabalistic techniques in the Torah.

Isaac	יצחק	Zohar	זוהר
Luria	לוריא	Kabbalah	קבלה

Some of the Masonic Symbols within Our Society

Different Satanic Symbols used in Freemasonry.

Fleur de Lis: Symbol of Ishtar, Goddess of Babylon

Fleur de Lis

Nike is Mercury: god of speed and Goddess of victory. The symbol is Saturn's ring.

Commemorative Masonic Postcard of man's arrival on the moon (1994).

Masonic Coin Commemorating the arrival of man on the moon.

The Obelisk is a symbol of the sun god, of the male energy and of the phallus.

Typical Clothing worn at lodges.

The Apron is part of the clothing worn by Masons throughout centuries.

Diverse symbols used inside the lodge.

Masonic Ring.

Diverse symbols used inside the lodge.

Figure of Christ with Masonic apron found in Catholic churches in Latin America.

Benito Juarez with Masonic apron.   *Stained glass window in Baptist Church.*

The Rosslyn Chapel is a church from the XV century located in the town of Rosslyn Midlothian, Scotland. Guillermo Saintclair, the first Count of Caithness, designed the chapel. A series of myths or legends have been weaved around the chapel. It is also said that it is a portal to another dimension. This chapel is used as a model for the construction of Masonic lodges all over the world.

Left: Pope John Paul VI doing the Masonic greeting.

Right: Pope Benedict XVI with the ex-Prime Minister of England, Tony Blair, performing the Masonic greeting.

The Masonic Greetings

The finger position of the hand is strategic at the moment to be identified. Political and religious leaders utilize this greeting.

Right: Notice the position of the fingers in a handshake greeting.

Below: The finger position varies in the different Masonic greetings according to the degrees.

Normal Greeting

Masonic Greetings

Masonic Greetings

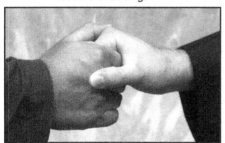

Masonic Greetings

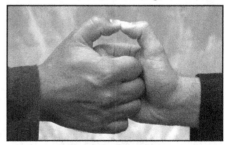

Masonic Greetings

Right: Nicolas Sarkozy, President of France and Moammar Quaddafi, President of Libia.

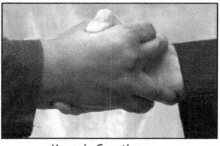

Masonic Greetings

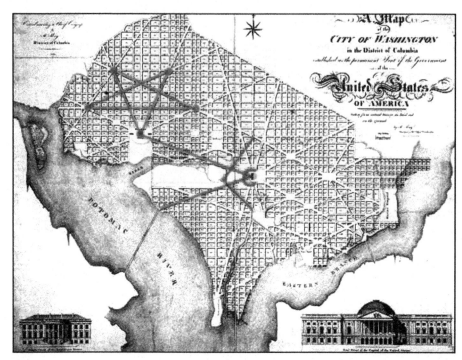

Design of Washington D.C. United States. This city is known for its series of building and monuments of Masonic origin that form a five-pointed star.

The Pentagon was built in the 1940's by General Leslie Groves, the same general who was in charge of the Manhattan Project which created the Atomic Bomb. According to the Masonic Conspiracy theory, General Groves was a FreeMason.

CHAPTER

MASONIC OATHS

A horrific part of the rites that is evident of the "directing mind" behind Freemasonry, are the dreadful oaths Masons have to submit to in each degree.

Jesus Christ said in the famous Sermon on the Mount:

"But I tell you, do not swear at all: either by heaven, for it is God's throne; or by the earth, for it is his footstool; or by Jerusalem, for it is the city of the Great King. And do not swear by your head, for you cannot make even one hair white or black. Simply let your 'Yes' be

'Yes,' and your 'No,' 'No'; anything beyond this comes from the evil one."   *Matthew 5:34-37*

When someone is interested in entering Freemasonry, or when Freemasonry takes an interest over an important candidate, he is never informed of what he is entering into. His thoughts are seduced with phrases like these:

"It is a voluntary association of free men. It is a system of moral conduct. It is a way of life. It is a fraternal society. It seeks to make men good and at times better. It teaches us morality through symbolism. It employs rites and ceremonies to instruct its members. It is based on the firm belief in the existence of a Superior Being, of the brotherhood and of the soul's immortality.

The candidate is assured that by belonging to this fraternity, his religious beliefs will be respected with ample tolerance; that he can be helped as many times as he needs by millions of Masons throughout the world; that he will meet and be a brother to the highest public figures in the world; and as a consequence, his life will be full of success from that point on. He is also told he will discover the most amazing truths about God, as he will become one of the chosen ones for the "Supreme Knowledge"; that his life will be full of satisfaction, by helping out in the welfare of the world, to save society, to overcome ignorance and carrying in his soul, the seal of being a world redeemer.

Having this beautiful string of lies as a lure, the candidate faces his first real great test, the one to strive for acceptance, or not. Of course, with such a marvelous expectation of his future life, who wouldn't be willing to confront anything to obtain it? It is in this way, the devil has sown his first seeds: ambition, greed and daring.

The candidate presents himself as a profane coming to seek the light of Freemasonry. He is asked for his general information and then in his first discourse, the Venerable Master who directs the ceremony, says among other things:

"The right of thinking and discussing, of believing or not believing, is based on knowledge, and on acting as reason dictates, and not according to the cunning or impulse of our first leaders. Know that the one who does not think or examine, the one who swears in the words of another and does not investigate if what he is taught and has been taught is true, is not a man, but is a machine. Doubt, my friend, what you do not understand or not know for yourself."

This is exactly what I am appealing to, your intellect, as you read this book. I want you to realize how Lucifer is weaving this monumental fraud and where its leading. To begin with, we see how the professed tolerance to the individual's religious beliefs has already been defiled, by giving rise to doubt and claiming that his first teachers are now obsolete and his decision to follow them was impulsive. Up to this point, the majority of the candidates haven't a clue as to what's happening. It may flutter in the backs of their minds that they are being invited to think, but they do not delve deeper into the ceremony. They have been told not to swear in the words of another and that is precisely what they are stealthily being led to do.

The interrogatory continues and the candidate is told what his duties are as a Mason. At this point, if he is willing to think, they should tell him clearly what Oaths he will take and the ceremonies he will participate in, so he would be able "to think" if he wants to go on or not. If they were upright, they would tell him, as stated by Albert Pike, that their doctrine is pure and totally Luciferian. It should be made clear that he will have to undergo mind control practices; that Freemasonry is intimately related to the ancient Mystical Order of Rosae-crucis and with the Orders of Knighthood, all of them, satanic orders.

It would be proper to tell him that out of these last mentioned, rose the most criminal rites of magic during the Middle Ages, such as the fearsome and obscure Order of the Templars, headed by Jacques de Molay. However, all of this is "too" secret, therefore the candidate is never warned. In the Magazine of the Supreme Council of Belgium, November 1, 1885, (pg. 44) Carlos Rahelemberck 33'rd degree said:

"We glorify the Templars, being their heirs, and we should do all we can as MEMBERS OF THIS SECRET TRIBUNAL. From the depths of its SECRET TRIBUNAL, Freemasonry of Belgium proposes to bring a revolution that will destroy social order through corruption and through the ANNIHILATION of Christianity, which is its official objective."

Do you think any of this is ever told to the "Christian" who penetrates the doors of Freemasonry?

Let's see what the presiding Venerable Master tells the aspiring candidate. Judge for yourself and think if this is right:

"Every association, my friend, has its laws, and every associate, his duties to perform; and as it would not be fair to impose obligations without you knowing what they are, it is prudent that this Respectable Association explain what your commitments are going to be.

1. There will be absolute silence about what you have heard, understood or discovered, and also what you will see and understand later on.

2. Your task is to fight the passions that bring dishonor to man, making him so vile, practicing charity, helping your brothers physically and emotionally, providing for their needs as much as possible and preventing their misfortunes, missing no opportunity to help them with your advice and light.

3. You will not know your duties until you have joined and these are to fulfill the general statutes of the Order, the constitutions of the Grand Lodge... and the particular regulations of this lodge, submitting yourselves to what is legally asked of you in its name, as we never prescribe anything unworthy of the honor and virtue we proclaim.

Now that you know the main obligations of a Mason, do

you think you have the strength and the firm, unfaltering resolution to practice them?"

This, beloved reader, is all a candidate is told, who following the "The huge lie", enters absolutely blinded to what awaits him in Freemasonry.

I want you to consider the deceitful clause about how a Mason will never be tasked to do anything unworthy of his honor. As a brief example, I want to cite a case whose scandal was known internationally. The financier Licio Gelli, a multifaceted man who had belonged to various political parties in Italy, in 1971, founded according to the official Italian Freemasonry, a famous lodge called "Propaganda 2". He developed it into a formidable hub of businesses, influence and mutual support among its members, who encompassed important figures from the Italian arenas of finance, politics, culture and the armed forces.

The influence extended even further to the other side of the Atlantic where a newspaper in Argentina published and article on it on September 15, 1982. There, the Lodge founded by Gelli was accused of kidnapping and revealing a state secret that produced a grave financial situation in the country. The article says as follows:

"The Fact was considered as a breach of a secret by Gelli himself having disclosed it. The final consequences are being investigated by Pedro Narvaiz's court, originating in the denouncement of the nationalist politician Patricio Kelly who accuses Gelli and the organization "P-2" of alleged interference in Argentine internal affairs and of provoking the current economic instability that the country is suffering."

There are hundreds of incidents like this one that have remained buried in Masonic silence. As you read the testimonies quoted in this book, you will get to know the extortion and horrific situations a mason has to endure. The Crimes and frauds Weishaupt used to keep members in bondage and silence, are everywhere in this association. Millions of Masons, some having an insatiable hunger for power, will do all kinds of things using the excuse that they needed to protect a fellow mason.

We would have to be extremely naïve to suppose that everything has been done on the level and in the open, when the Order is linked to every world government and to believe no one has ever done anything shady to cover a brother Mason, or to save him from an oppressor.

Let's return to the initiation. After the Venerable Master reads the ambiguous obligations to the candidate and advises him never to swear in the words of another, he leads him in the following oath. (Irony of ironies).

"Layman, before moving forward, we require our oath upon the book of the Law (Bible). Do you swear?" If the candidate accepts, then the Venerable continues, "Repeat after me: I... give my word of honor, to comply with the obligations of a good Mason, and I declare that it is not curiosity that led me here, but the love of progress. And, if I lie, I permit that just as the sweetness of this drink (he has to drink sweet water) is changed to bitterness, (he has to drink bitter water) the water that I drink would change to poison, and the scorn of men and the curse of the Great Architect of the Universe would fall upon my head."

This candidate, who knows nothing of the depths of Freemasonry, has just sworn and sentenced himself directly to lucifer with a curse placed upon his head. He doesn't even know if he is going to agree with the things that follow, or what all of this represents for the latter destiny of his soul.

After this Oath, he proceeds to the three initiate's journeys, where he will penetrate the spiritual dimensions of hell. In the next chapter, I will narrate this experience vividly. He will have to come in totally blindfolded, without being informed at all about the consequences of what he is about to do.

When the journey's concluded, he has to sign a document with his eyes still blindfolded and without having the slightest idea of what the written document contains. From testimonies I have gathered, this paper has the written confession of an abominable crime for which the aspirant has just claimed to be responsible. In one case that I personally heard of, they made the candidate sign a confession to kidnapping, murder and the sale of organs of over one hundred children. When the person reads what he has signed, he faints from anguish. The initiate is subjected to a mock trial in which he is found guilty and is sentenced to death by means of terrible tortures.

Once the sentence is given, the Venerable nails the document onto a sword and burns it, telling the initiate that in spite of his guilt, Freemasonry pardons him, if he signs with his own blood, an unbreakable covenant of solidarity with the order.

This oath is denominated as sacred. The Venerable speaks again and says: "My friend, you must take an even more sacred oath, and this oath must be signed in your own blood. Tell us if you want us to make you bleed and in what part of your body." After the aspirant agrees, the Venerable continues:

"Your resolution is enough and grace is bestowed upon you. Brother Experts, lead the layman to the altar of oaths and accompany me, my Brother servants."

"My friend, repeat after me," continues the Venerable Master. "I.... of my own free will, before the Great Architect of the Universe and this respectable association, do solemnly swear and promise in good faith, to never reveal any of the secrets, acts or mysteries that I have seen today or that may later be told to me, except to another Mason. I swear not to write, record, engrave, trace, print, or form any character or sign by which the Sacred Word may be known and its means of communication among the Masons be revealed.

I would rather have my throat slit and my tongue pulled out from the root. I swear to help my brothers, as far as my strength allows and to be loyal and chaste with their wives, brothers, mothers and daughters. If you do this, God will help you and if not, God will find you guilty."

In this manner, the candidate becomes fraudulently bound by satan to something he doesn't even have knowledge of. Anyone having a covenant with Jesus Christ, or with Jehovah the Father, has just broken it by entering the dominion and lordship of this sun god, Osiris or the Great Architect of the Universe. Whoever tries to follow both paths should not deceive themselves. Jehovah does not share His glory with anyone. The book of Hebrews says:

"We must pay more careful attention, therefore, to what we have heard, so that we do not drift away. For if the message spoken by angels was binding, and every violation and disobedience received its just punishment, how shall we escape if we ignore such a great salvation? This salvation, which was first announced by the Lord, was confirmed to us by those who heard him. God also testified to it by signs, wonders and various miracles, and signs of the Holy Spirit distributed according to his will."

Hebrews 2:1-4

Don't believe, beloved reader, that the true God who sent His Son to die for our sins, will consider anyone innocent who makes oaths with lucifer or with a foreign god, and even more so, if he knows the Gospel. He said:

"And the Lord said to Moses: "You are going to rest with your fathers, and these people will soon prostitute

themselves to the foreign gods of the land they are entering. They will forsake me and break the covenant I made with them."   *Deuteronomy 31:16*

And if you reject my decrees and abhor my laws and fail to carry out all my commands and so violate my covenant...
                                                   Leviticus 26:15

It is possible to break the covenants of Freemasonry and undo its oaths. I will discuss it at the end of this book.

CHAPTER

REAL TESTIMONIES OF INITIATIONS

Everything I have expounded to this point has been the result of a profound investigation into the Masonic Order. However, it is necessary to include amongst these pages, true testimonies from people who have been involved in Freemasonry. For this, I sought out an old friend Tanya, who like myself, had in the past, been involved in a series of occult philosophies and branches of parapsychology..

Additionally, she had entered the sinister world of Freemasonry, reaching the highest degree a woman can achieve: the third one.

She renounced Freemasonry to truly serve Christ, surrendering her life to Him to preach the unique Gospel of the Cross.

When I asked her to help me with this book, her eyes lit up, brimming with an enormous satisfaction, as if she had always wanted to do something like this. She saw the sun rising over a yearning kept away for a long time.

Interview with Tanya

-Ana: Tanya, how can someone become a Mason? Had the Masons sought after you or did you find them?

-Tanya: Freemasonry is highly secret. In fact, it is not easy to discover a Mason or to get close to them. Everything is handled based on secret codes, such as touches, signals and absolutely confidential words.

They don't seek you out unless you are a very important person or if you can serve a specific plan they have in mind. In most cases, one seeks them, seduced precisely by that mysterious and occult character that emanates from the way they handle their affairs.

It's the aura of mystery, which surrounds them that attracts the soul of man who is seeking to fill that inner void he has tried to fill by every possible means with no results.

Others join The Order seeking to obtain relationships

with important people or in an ambitious search for power. In order to get in, you need to make contact with one of its members and practically beg him to help you obtain an application. Once you get it, it's submitted to a trial by which they accept you or not.

-Ana: Personally, what were you looking for? Why did you believe it was so important to join this society?

-Tanya: At that time I was very involved with esoterism and parapsychology, but inside of me was a yearning to have an encounter with God, and that was the hook. In those environments, what they use to attract the unwary is the affirmation that God is hidden for most people and only a few find Him. This is logical because I now know man can never reach God, it is God himself who seeks us and calls us back to Himself. At the time, I was desperately looking for those heavenly places that occult sciences constantly talk about.

I wanted by all means to feel a fullness with God that could satisfy my inner need. I was irresistibly drawn to them upon learning that they worshipped the one I thought was the true God, the Great Architect of the Universe, the supreme God. I was delighted by the fact that over there, His wisdom and His knowledge were sought at any cost, but in my ignorance I didn't know how far God was from this Association, apparently so full of Him.

Anyone who is in this search is an easy prey for Freemasonry. Its appearance of nobility and of goodness is satan's greatest ruse to overwhelm the ego with dainties, entangle man's soul and drag him to his eternal abyss.

It's incredible to watch how people accept anything with such ease if it possesses a minimum of logic. It's more comfortable to accept the digested plate, than to get into the tedious chore of proving if it comes from God or not.

We become satisfied as long as the teachings and theories imparted to us make sense according to our criteria. We allow ourselves to be deceived, without realizing that we could naively be getting into the very jaws of hell itself. At times, I have thought about how little we appreciate our soul and how little fear there is in this world about our eternal destiny. We think we are the owners of life and death; becoming ruthless judges, trying to remove the straw from another's eye and not seeing the beam that blinds us. How much pain would I have saved myself from, if I had inquired of God in His Word and obeyed it with a meek and trustful heart!"

How truthful it was with everything Tanya said. I remained silent, meditating a moment and then continued.

A Real Trip to Hell

-Ana: Once they accepted your application, what was the initiation ceremony like?

-Tanya: "It was nighttime. A hooded man greeted me on the street at the door of the lodge. This person is known as the

First Expert. He blindfolded me and guided me through the lodge; after a number of turns, he led me into the reflection room. There, he removed the blindfold. It was a black room with a table, a casket and some other objects. In a thick, slow voice he told me to reflect on everything I was seeing and to complete the form on the table written on a triangular sheet of paper. Afterwards, he left the room, instructing me that when I finished, I should knock three times on the table and not turn around to see who came in.

The dark room was barely illuminated by some candles, which made the casket and a skull in the table gleam in a sinister manner. On the walls there were drawn symbols of death. The first thing I thought about was my own death, on my own passing away, the fleeting nature of life and how important it is to be prepared for our eternal destiny. I wanted to be at peace with God, so the only thing that occurred to me was to ask for forgiveness of my sins and also beg for His protection for this unknown ceremony I was going to undertake.

I never asked Him whether it was pleasing to Him or not in what I was doing. I presumptuously assumed that He had to help me in whatever circumstance I was in because I saw Him as a God of love, without considering He is also Just and Holy. I was too conceited in my own reasoning to ask His opinion, or perhaps I knew Him so little that I figured He was too busy to pay any attention to me. The things one thinks! The truth is that He is an Omnipresent God, Almighty and He is attentive to the work of His hands. Where could I hide that He couldn't hear me or for Him not to see me? When I finished writing, I did as I had been commanded and it wasn't long before I heard the doorknob squeak behind me.

Once again I felt unknown hands putting the blindfold over my eyes, and they took me outside the Lodge again. They had me untuck my shirttail and roll up my left sleeve and bound my left hand with a scarf tied to my neck. Then they raised the pant leg of my right leg and ordered me to leave all my money outside. All this, symbolized the spiritual, emotional and physical state in which I was arriving, to ask help from Freemasonry and to receive what they call your first light: Naked, barefoot, disabled, blind and poor.

They were questioning me exhaustively about my religious beliefs, when someone started to knock on the outside door in an irregular pattern. The "Inner Temple Guard" was alerted. Several voices shouted from inside: "Alarm, they are knocking profanely at the temple door!". Another strong, deep voice shouted, "Who is the risk taker that dares to interrupt our work and tries to force open the doors of the temple?" In that moment, a mild air current was felt coming from the door slightly opened. I felt the urge to step forward when the point of a sword stopped me leveled at the height of my heart.

The hooded man:-"Stop! I am the one who introduces this profane woman to our Respectable Association."

The sword was then lowered. Still blind folded, I was introduced to the Venerable Master who instead of welcoming me, raised his voice and said, sending a chill up my spine:

Venerable Master–"Friends, take up your swords, a profane woman is at the doors of the temple."

A loud sound of steel was heard that was instantly silenced by the Venerable.

Venerable Master: -"Brother Expert, what is your intention of binging her here? What do you expect?"

Hooded man:- "That a woman of honor, although a profane one, be admitted among us."

Venerable Master:-"What gives her the right to deserve it?

Hooded man:-"The right of being a free woman of good manners. I vouch for her."

After asking me about my general information, the "Venerable Master" gave a speech about the state of darkness they were receiving me in and how the genius of evil made me an instrument of discord and misfortune. He said that this darkness I was immersed in, was the image of an ignorant who automatically obeys his impulses, just like the hand that was now leading me around. He exhorted me to think about everything I was told and to doubt anything I did not understand or did not know to be true. He then concluded by saying:

Venerable Master:-"Reflect well on the consequences of the step you are about to take, because they are terrible and hideous for the weak who is overwhelmed by their weight, and only the person of faith and valor can resist them and be victorious. If you lack those virtues, tremble, because your sacrifice is immense and the tests that you will endure can wear out your steadfastness and shake your resolve. If you enter our ranks, you will not only have to fight tooth and nail like we do, during your lifetime against our natural enemies, "Passions", but also against even more hidden enemies; against all hypocrites, all fanatics, all the greedy, ignorant or learned, against all who speculate with ignorance and the darkness of men, their brothers. Do you feel you have enough energy to be a member of our association and are you committed to supporting the work that you will endure during the rest of your existence in this battle of light against darkness, of Honor against Treachery, of Truth against Error?"

When he finished his discourse, he read to me the duties of the Mason and they took me to the Venerable's throne to take my first oath. They had me drink water with honey and then bitter water. Afterwards he gave me plain water, and this meant that the water I would drink from the moment I lied would change to poison and the curse of the Great Architect of the Universe would be upon me. When I finished it, they removed the blindfold from my eyes. On the table in front of me was a sheet of paper, so the Venerable put a pen in my hands and with a commanding, firm voice said: "Sign here!". I hesitated a moment because I didn't want to sign anything without knowing what it was, at that moment he slightly nudged my shoulder as if to encourage me, and I did it. Then, the Venerable said to the hooded man leading me:

-"Prepare all the utensils for the tests; the water, the fire, the basin for the blood and the rest of the utensils."

They blindfolded me again, while in my mind I was questioning full of horror what those instruments would be used for. I couldn't see anything. Countless conflicting emotions raged within me. I was afraid, but I tried with all my might to muster all the courage I had ever held. One phrase incessantly pounded within me, "You must pass the test, Tanya, you must pass it, only then will you be accepted." On the other hand, I cried to God to give me strength, praying the Lord's Prayer, over and over again. It was not only a test to be accepted in the initiation but also for me, to know if all that power I had acquired in New Age, to help others was as real as I had boasted of. What was I getting myself into? I asked myself. Was this the only way to get to my beloved God?

The time came to begin the first journey. Everything was dark. Not even the most remote string of light could be perceived through the blindfold. Something inside me told me that this wasn't good. They left me alone for a while in that dark place with one hand and one leg raised. The place was damp and cold. My heart beat was accelerating. I was very nervous. I didn't know where they were taking me, and while facing the unknown, fear grabbed hold of my imagination, becoming my worst enemy. After some minutes that seemed an eternity, "the journey" began. Someone took me by my hand and lead me. A grim and mysterious music sounded in the background. A breeze was blowing as the guide carefully led me along a stone path, saying:

-"There is a precipice in front of us, this is the valley of the dead, walk slowly and carefully; the path is very narrow."

The air began striking with greater force and I was invaded by the terrible sensation that a void was opening beneath my feet. A vertigo pounding at my stomach made me feel like the abyss was pulling me in and was dragging me downwards. Perhaps we were circling a deep cistern or the excavation for the foundation of some large building. I recalled Dante alligieri's "The Divine Comedy" with the whirlwind that never ceases to spin formed by the lost souls on their way to Hell. I had the impression of seeing their faces disfigured by their anguish and desperation, fall with acceleration into the emptiness of the depths.

The ground was sandy, which made it difficult for me to walk with firm, sure steps. Beside that, adding to my fright was the horrible sensation of stepping on someone's hand as they were eagerly grabbing unto the parapet in a desperate and futile attempt to escape from their infernal agony. Suddenly, my guide stopped cold, as if he were trying to cover me from something that had left him speechless. The imagination in that darkness and under those circumstances was firing away at me, creating living forms between the unreal and the real and even more, by having heard that Masons are capable of anything. The music abruptly stopped with a sonorous organ blast. The wind was still blowing strongly, but it could not muffle the thundering roar that was heard. Victimized by panic, I clung unto a rock on the road.

The roars continued vibrating in the throat of what I identified to be an enormous feline. The stealthy crawling of its claws made me think that he would pounce on us in a matter of seconds. They made it so real, believe me!

Suddenly, something voluminous fell on me, knocking the air out of me. At the same time, the guide jerked me forcefully and we crashed against what I supposed were some rocks that scraped all my ribs. Voices and blows were then heard and it was at that moment that the hand of my guide got me up. The noise was very loud, as if we were in the middle of an earthquake or an avalanche. The thundering noise continued for a while and then it began easing down until there was total silence. What have I gotten myself into, I thought.

With the blindfold still on, we found ourselves in front of the Venerable Master, who explained the meaning of the First Journey:

-"The obstacles you have stumbled upon and that would have made you fall if you had not been guided by an expert hand, represent the first stage of life with all its impotence against error and the cunning of men, against that world you came from, bristling with hurdles, where without teachers, your ignorance would crash you down. In the initiation, this journey also represents the second element, air, with its noises, thunder and disorder. You would have noticed that after that noise, there came a perfect calm, likewise in the same manner after a hurricane and nature's cataclysms, comes a rest. Once the time, or the age of error and doubt are over with, one enjoys tranquility, reasoning and the peace of the soul that satisfies the conscience."

I would like to pause a moment from Tanya's encounter to cite the explanation Master Leadbeater gives about this journey. He says that it represents a weak imitation of the tests that the candidate had to endure in the old Mysteries, when he was led past eerie caverns, a symbol of the lower astral world; among tumultuous noises and surrounded by dangers he could not understand. The Master adds that "for those who join into the Masonic order, after death they must pass through the lower sub-plane of the astral world that they should be prepared to endure the test calmly and without fear." What Leadbeater is saying concretely, is that those who may be going to the most terrible parts of hell for their eternal destiny must begin training themselves here. I have no comment!

Continuing now with her initiation:

–Tanya: As we arrived at a second portal, we approached what I found out was the seat of honor of the Second Watchman. Here, they introduced me to the spirits of the earth and water belonging to the Astral region that we were entering in. Still blindfolded, I was lead to a place full of little critters I was squashing under my feet. "Jump!" shouted my guide. "It is full of spiders and vipers." Their sound slithering over the floor could be heard in between the discordant musical notes they were now playing. I tried to shake them off of me, throwing my legs about and endeavoring to barely touch the ground with my bare foot. I was shivering as I felt the arachnid's light and tiny legs slide down my blouse. I felt like running and screaming. But, run where? Cry out to whom? It was as if I were entering hell itself. My only point of trust was the unknown hand that led me and that solemn voice that warned me of the dangers. For a moment, I thought how absurd all this was, so foreign from everything my conscience understood as being good. In hindsight, I know today that there is only one power that would be interested in training us for eternal hell and that is satan.

We continued onward to where a humid swamp, covered by putrefied vapors, was our next step. In the background, anguished, faltering voices could be heard. The music seemed like languid moans that floated in the air like voices from the otherworld, crying out to be freed of their torment. Underneath my feet, I felt like I was walking through a quagmire where pieces of branches and gravel made it rough at times and stabbing at others. I felt something scrape my bare leg but I did not have time to think about what it was because in that moment the voice warned me:

Guide:-"Be careful! Crouch down low and walk slowly. Above us is a huge Python snake. He is not looking at us intently, but he senses we are here. We must make him think that he has a lot of time to attack because once he fixes his gaze on us, he will strike so he can choke us."

We walked very slowly. Something cold touched my back, as if it were a long hand that slid through the breadth of my ribs. I stopped breathing. My heartbeats were rising by the minute. I was so tense it was dulling my movements more and more. There was the sound of rustling foliage and it felt as if the gaze of some being watched us and was following us, waiting for the exact moment to come out and meet up with us. Perhaps it was one gaze that hunted us stealthily, but I felt thousands of eyes piercing my body and not knowing their purpose gave me goose bumps. Maybe they were the desperate looks from those trying to tell me they were never able to leave that place; that they were forever trapped in hell and that there was no longer any hope. The heart-wrenching cry from their entrails no longer finds an echo in that almost imperceptible divine presence one feels when lifting up a plea unto heaven. Their souls can only hear the void, the eternal emptiness where their voices are lost, the torment of being forever separated from God. This thought shook my consciousness, but I had no time to reflect deeply on it.

Guide:-"We are entering the land of mandrills. Though the trees are tall and lush, we must walk calmly so they won't be afraid, they need to know we are friendly."

He had not finished the sentence when the dull thud of several of them dropping to the ground left me paralyzed. I felt their breathing close to me. One of them hung from my shirt and began shaking me. His nails sunk into my back and his breathing down my neck made me think the end had come. He shook me around with such force that I fell to the ground. Growls and a commotion were heard as if they were fighting among themselves to see who would devour our flesh. I couldn't handle it anymore. I was fear's captive and I was about to pull the blindfold off when a long, distant moan stopped me, which I thought came from someone who had failed the test.

Suddenly, I heard the sound of falling water and the mandrills ran away. We found ourselves in a hot, humid place that smelled like smoke. The lamentations became louder along with dragging chains. The music that was still heard began to accelerate its rhythm, as if something was about to surprise us in any moment. I felt like my heart was going to jump out of my throat in an instant. It seemed as if we had entered the bottomless pit. There was the loud noise of steel clanging against iron, like the sound of a sword crashing against an anvil. My mind had transported to the throne of Vulcan, that incandescent underground cave where the crippled, herculean god of fire and metallurgy forged the arms of the Roman gods.

A stifling heat was felt and at the same time an obscure spiritual presence became tangible, as if a winged, enormous black shadow, deeper than night itself, ruled that place. In spite of the steep temperature that was asphyxiating us, my bones could sense that fearsome spirit like an icy knife piercing them with a sharp pain. The sound of the metals clashing became clear. It was a duel with swords.

A battle similar to the one resounding within me; my own struggle for survival. It was a duel between my own beliefs that amidst the confusion and chaos, were still trying to continue existing in this unbearable war between good and evil. "The only thing I desire is to find my God!" I shouted, and my voice seemed to get lost in an unfathomable void that filled my whole inner being. How far can the soul take flight, or to what deep abysses can the invisible specters of deep darkness drag it into? How do you stop the rampant and frenzied advancement of terror? Where does good vanish to in this murky fog where evil disguises itself as good? Where does reality end and illusion and raving begin? Who moves the soul's strings, to thrust them forward like a tempestuous wave between one rock and the other. Where are you, oh God? And, where is, this humble profane woman, who so seeks you?

We continued the course. He made me raise one leg to jump over a rock and when I came down, we had entered what seemed like a river. We walked for a while through the water and then we got out of it. We did this three times. Then we entered a reflection room, where I would spend long hours during my Masonic career. They removed the blindfold and told me to write my will. This seemed suspicious and filled me with fear. Especially since there was a casket in front of me, which could very well be my next destination if I did not pass the test. I thought about it at that moment; although at the same time, I doubted they could go that far. I was unaware of the diabolic spider web that was being woven, covering my entire being and from which many never escape. I knew that those who cross the threshold of Freemasonry, open a door that is only bolted on the outside and that he who has entered can't go back.

When I finished writing my final wishes in full detail, the guide returned and put the blindfold back on to continue our course. He led me to a chair in front of a table and told me to sit down. The Venerable Master then spoke to me explaining the second journey.

Venerable Master:-"Of the difficulties you have suffered, the water you have passed through is the bronze sea, allegoric of the earth. The noise of swords represent, on the one hand, the second age of life, whose passions are like stormy waves, and the clash of steel signals our tendency to become judges and executioners. On the other hand, it also represents our victory over the third element, water."

According to the explanation that Leadbeater gives of this journey, the candidate is on a pilgrimage through the regions ruled by the elemental spirits and is on the way to the path of the upper planes.

Venerable Master:-"After death, those who clung to the inferior degree of emotional existence incorporating themselves in such class of matter, must remain in the lower sub-planes of the astral world. The second journey is analogous to the first one, with the difference that the sounds are softer and less thunderous. The candidate is still in the astral world, but in the intermediate part, much more refined and subtle than the one he just passed through. This is the region of the blind passions; the one of ordinary human emotions."

They blindfolded me again and we began the third journey. A loud sound of flames and an intense heat was felt, my guide tried to bring me close to the fire, but I was too frightened. "There is no alternative, you must cross!" I covered my face with my bandaged arm, and mustering up my courage, I allowed my guide to drag me through what I imagined would be a glowing wall. We crossed that hell. The roar of the flames became more and more faint giving way to soft music. We walked slowly. We encountered two other series of flames, which we crossed without any setbacks, and this is how this last journey concluded. They seated me again and the Venerable explained its meaning.

Venerable Master:-"In this journey, my friend, only one man stopped you, representing mature age. The flames you passed through represent your purification and love for your fellow men that must eternally burn in your heart. You have concluded the three journeys established since remote ancient times. The lustral water you bathed in carried in its current the dregs of your past ages, just as the fire consumed your former vices, so that the memory from that corruption would be lost."

According to Lavagnini's Learning Manual[1], in the old

Mysteries, this journey represented the entrance to a restful region, symbol of the upper sub-planes of the astral world.

-Tanya: -Upon ending the journey, they seated me in front of a table upon which they placed another paper and told me to sign it without reading it. I didn't want to sign anything without knowing what it was. With insistence, they encouraged me to do it, without physically forcing me. Thinking that it might be my certificate of acceptance to the Order, I took the pen and signed the document.

It was then when they removed the blindfold from my eyes. Before me rose a majestic parlor, covered with the finest carved wood with a series of symbols, squares, compasses and swords. The ceiling was painted a deep blue, with a firmament full of stars and signs of the zodiac. At the back, in front of the portico, were two imposing columns with some serpents coiled around them, carved from the same wood and painted as if they were of bronze. Between them was a beautiful picture that represented a rainbow and the whole large room was lit only with candles, lending to it a sinister aspect, while at the same time, mysteriously attractive.

All along the walls were seated the companions and apprentices, all wearing their work apron tied at the waist. In front of me, in the middle of the room, was the "Ara", the Masonic altar, upon which was placed a red pillow with an open Bible and over it a square, a compass and some swords.

All of this symbolized that reasoning should rule over the

body and the spirit.

The few instants they allowed me to be in silence gazing upon the place, were interrupted by the grave voice of the Venerable Master, who proceeded to read the document I had signed in a paused manner. I don't remember the exact words he was saying, but I will never forget the chill that ran through my body and the terror of seeing myself beyond escape. I realized that what I had signed was my direct involvement in a crime in which I was accusing myself of having committed. I felt lost like a shipwreck survivor in the middle of the ocean buffeted around during a storm. Now, I was really alone and without a way out.

Immediately after the reading, a trial was organized against me. My confession was decisive to their declaring me guilty and practically without any deliberation, I was sentenced to be skinned alive and to be chopped up into pieces afterwards.

From what I had heard about the power of Masonry, it didn't seem far fetched that they could make me disappear and justice wouldn't lift a finger to investigate it. It is such a powerful organization! I thought that everything that had happened was a cruel mask to find a guilty one for a crime they had committed, so they could wash their hands of it with impunity. They set me up and I had no hope.

Overtaken by the deepest despair, I waited in agony for that whole nightmare to end. Then, they pulled out another paper and placed it before me. I was terrified to know what it contained. My whole body shook. The Venerable raised his voice in the somber silence:

Venerable Master: -"Exercising love and brotherhood, the pillars of our Order, we have decided to forgive your life and to protect you from justice for this infamy you have committed, in exchange, you owe us your life perpetually in order to serve the ends of Freemasonry and to help any brother Mason you may find in any difficulty. To this end, you will sign the covenant of honor and acceptance to the brotherhood in your own blood, which you swear never to betray, or reveal its secrets, or the touches that will be taught to you, so you identify yourself and to enter the lodge, or the word of power that today we present to you as a special treasure of your degree.

Now, tell us: On what part of your body do you prefer to be made to bleed?"

I extended my arm for them to extract the blood for the pact to be sealed with, as I was surrendering my life in service to Freemasonry.

Venerable Master:-"Your resolution is enough for me and grace is made for you. Brother Expert, lead the profane woman to the Ara of Oaths," added the Venerable.

When I had signed, the Venerable asked for a sword. A woman gave it to him. With the gesture of someone doing something heroic, he pierced the document with the sword that charged me and holding it on high, set it on fire.

Then, they took me to the reflection room to fix my clothing and return to the temple with my eyes again blindfolded. When the Venerable asked the two Watchmen and the Orator, who had been my keepers and defenders, what they wanted for me, They answered in unison, "Light, the Great Light." Then the voice of the Venerable was heard, parodying the voice of God in the miraculous act of the "Fiat Lux", saying:

Venerable Master:-"Let there be light."

Only then, did they remove my blindfold for good. I was surrounded by all of my new "brothers". With their arms raised, each one held an unsheathed sword forming a sort of flashing dome over me.

In Aldo Lavagnini's Learning Manual, referring to this moment, he says:

-"The brothers gathered around the aspirant, with their swords together forming a steel vault above his head, without him still becoming aware of their presence with his own eyes, they are the symbol of those presences or invisible intelligences that constantly surround us, without our knowledge; mute witnesses of our acts, that watch us, protect us, and help us so we can carry out our purposes and our highest aspirations."

Tanya:- "They lowered their swords and forming a circle inter-locking their arms with each other, they said with one voice, "All for one and one for all."

The ceremony ended with my consecration to the Great Architect of the Universe and upon completion, everyone approached me to embrace me and to congratulate me for having been accepted into the fraternity. I was dazed by exhaustion after so many hours of terror and befuddled by a strange sense of happiness for having accomplished it. I couldn't realize that there was not only a party occurring in an earthly lodge, but the real celebration was being carried out in the supreme Lodge of the prince of darkness, where my name had just been inscribed with my own blood. How could I imagine, amidst hugs and well wishes, that it was satan to whom I had actually surrendered my soul to, and along with it, my eternal destiny."

Testimony of David W.M. Vaughan of the Great Lodge of London

Initiation of the Third Degree

"The basis for the ceremony of third degree is a representation of the history of the death of the Masonic Master Hiram Abiff. According to the story, he was brutally tortured by three vile workers because he refused to reveal the secrets of his high degree Master Mason. He was struck on the head with a wooden mallet (masonry hammer) leading to his death. During the ceremony, the candidate is also symbolically struck on the forehead and is laid on the floor of the lodge, this simulating the death of Hiram."

"The story continues with the Master's remains mysteriously disappearing. When his body is finally found after seven days, various attempts are made to resuscitate him. First, the Apprentice tries, raising him by one hand, but he slips and is unsuccessful; then a companion tries, but has the same result. Finally, a more expert worker tries, supporting the body strongly using his right hand.

He comes to life, after touching him in the five key points of companionship. The Masonic Rite says, simulating a resurrection "Hand with hand, I greet you as brother; feet with feet I will sustain you in your praiseworthy commitments; knee with knee, the pose of my daily supplications, I will remember your desires; chest with chest, when you trust me with a secret I will keep it as if it were my own; and hand upon back I will protect your honor in your absence and in your presence."

"These sentiments seemed at the time like a wonderful way of declaring one Mason's concern for another. Frankly," David adds, "it is very easy to accept these ideals, and if the whole world were to adopt them, humanity would be something else. But it is also so easy to be led by the superficial value of these words and not completely see the terrible heresy behind the ceremony."

Certificate of Third Degree Master Mason Initiation.

"This portion of the ritual where I had to play out my symbolic death and resurrection, took place in the reflection room under very dim light. They put me in a coffin with an acacia branch in my hands and put next to me, a human skull and some bones that symbolized death and told me, 'The light of a Master Mason is **Visible Darkness**.' The meaning of these obscure words made me realize much later that it was none other than the light of satan, the prince of darkness." David W.V. Vaughan

For most of the people initiated in this degree, this ceremony is no more than a reflection upon death and a dramatic representation of the death of this ancient architect of Solomon's Temple. In theory, the spiritual context of this ceremony is taken from the teaching that Jesus Christ gives to Nicodemus:

"In reply Jesus declared, "I tell you the truth, unless a man is born again, he cannot see the kingdom of God." "How can a man be born when he is old?" Nicodemus asked. "Surely he cannot enter a second time into his mother's womb to be born!" Jesus answered, "I tell you the truth, unless a man is born of water and the Spirit, he cannot enter the kingdom of God. Flesh gives birth to flesh, but the Spirit gives birth to spirit."   John 3:3-6

This is a portion of Scripture widely used in initiation settings to represent the aspirant's entrance into the spiritual world.

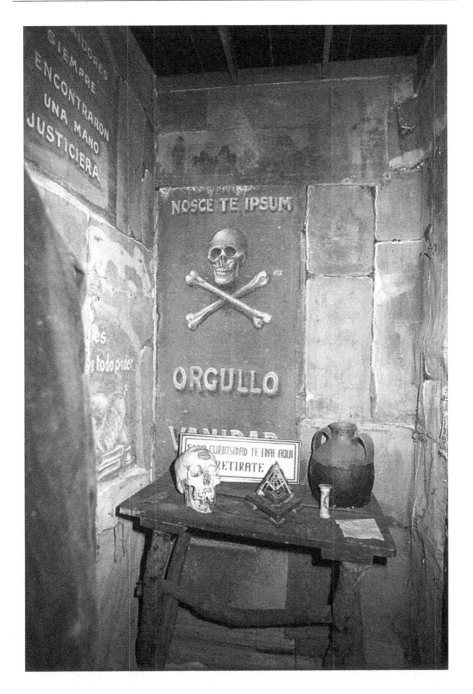

Reflexion Room into which the Aspirant enters blindfolded. Upon exiting, after performing a series of covenant, he will see the "light".

Unfortunately, the Bible is used to afford a more serious nature to the ceremony. The person feels more secure, when finding in the Word of God, something similar to the rite being carried out. To participate in a ritual where Death comes into play would not be easy to accept if it were not softened with God's apparent approval. However, as noted previously, the True and Only God does not take part of a ceremony simply because it mentions His name. He only acts through what He has established and in the manner He has decreed. In the verse cited from John, Jesus is speaking of the believer who makes the decision to invoke His Spirit, with a sincere attitude of making Him the Lord of his life. In the Masonic realm, the so-called "Death Initiation" is a well-known ceremony celebrated in ancient Egypt.

This ritual is not in any way a harmless teaching that makes us reflect upon our latter destiny, nor is it a theatrical representation of the murder of Hiram Abiff. It is however, an important doorway to penetrate into the dimension of darkness.

In this ritual, the aspirant is turned over to the spirit of Death by getting into a casket. The acacia branch that he holds over his chest symbolizes the "Conceiving Phallus" through which he receives luciferian energy.

In ancient times, the initiate was surrendered to Anubis, who was resuscitated by the power of Osiris. This giving of life represents the solar cycle, which begins its decline in autumn, ends up dying in winter and is reborn stronger in spring. The legend says that Osiris was betrayed by Typhon, after having traveled the universe and was resuscitated by Anubis, the god of death, who brought him back to life with renewed vigor on the summer solstice, June 24th (one of Freemasonry's key dates).

The third degree initiation ceremony is really an invocation to be inhabited by the power and spirit of Death.

A salutation of congratulations after undergoing the process of initiation at the Masonic Lodge.

The Great Secretary of the Supreme Council for the Southern Jurisdiction says regarding about this initiation:

"Typhon killed Osiris, putting him in a casket. Immediately he divided his body into several pieces and threw them in the Nile. Osiris' widow Isis searched for his remains and found them, except for his "membrum virile". In memory of this loss, the worship of the "phallus" was instituted because it is only through it that reproduction is possible."

The Masons find this phallus in the degree of master or third degree, under the designation of the word Mahabone.[2] However, just as physical laws affect us relentlessly, even if we are unaware of them, spiritual laws also affect us whether we know about them or not.

It is remarkable how all over the world, there is a great lack of knowledge about the spiritual world and about how our spirit is affected, frequently without us realizing it. I want to illustrate this with the following example: A person enters a hospital for contagious illnesses, touching everything he sees, taking no precautions, ignorant of the true nature of the place and his skin is accidently pierced with a used syringe. This person did not mean to become infected, but whether he wanted to or not, he will leave this place with a terrible virus circulating throughout his body.

Our soulish and emotional aspects are equally prone to contagions, be it voluntary or not. How many of us, for example, have seen a movie that has touched the weakest and most sensitive areas of our soul and we have been affected to a greater degree after it's over?

Well then, if these cases of "contagions" are possible and real, for the body as well as for the soul, what makes us assume that the spirit can't also be affected when we submit it to spiritual experiences of this magnitude?

In the third degree exegesis made by Master C.W. Leadbeater, it mentions:

"In the third degree as in others, the candidate kneels underneath a triangle while the blessing of the Almighty is invoked (name that is given in this degree to the Great Architect of the Universe). It is worth mentioning that in Freemasonry all the oaths are performed inside this same triangle, a sign that the entire triune man, body, soul and spirit, is taking part in the work."

Perhaps the aspirant is fully conscious of what is happening in his body and he may meditate about what his emotions and feelings have endured during the macabre process of this initiation, but you can be sure that he will be totally ignorant of what may have happened in the more subtle and defenseless part of all his being, his spirit. With the individual left defenseless and unaware "spiritually", of what is happening to him, the prince of darkness, the "visible darkness" that has been invoked, will not miss this opportunity to penetrate and shackle his spirit.

Notes

1. *Translation from Aldo Lavagnini: Manual of the Apprentice. (Spanish Original Title: El Manuel del Aprendiz)*
   2. *Lexicon of Freemasonry by Albert Jorge Mackey, pg. 249.*

CHAPTER

THE RITE OF THE GREAT ORIENT OF FRANCE

The Masonic Rite of the Great Orient of France is a clear example of spiritual infiltration and domination. In this Rite, the veiled disguise of an organization with a charitable purpose, has been ripped off in a cynical and brutal manner.

Its true origins and goals against the "system," any form of religion and every attempt to approach God are crudely exposed. In particular, its third degree initiation using the disguise of the dramatic reenactment of Hiram Abiff's murder, along with his three executioners, to impregnate the soul of the new "Master" with the "real" Masonic spirit. The Instruction committee, led by the Rite's Supreme Council says:

"The order must remain immaculate and inaccessible to suspicion. The order is the Great Revenger of the murdered Grand Master, isn't its role, the Great Avenger of Humanity?"

"The innocent Grand Master, you have felt him, he is the Man who is King and Lord of the Grand Nature; the man who is born innocent, since he is born unconscious."

"Our innocent Grand Master was born to be happy; to enjoy in all its fullness, all his rights without exception. But he fell under the blows of three assassins, three infamous cads who lifted formidable obstacles to his well-being and his rights and who finally annihilate him. These three murders are: **The Law, Property and Religion**."

"The Law, because it is the perfect harmony between the rights of the isolated Man and the duties of social man in society. Property, because the land does not belong to anyone; being its resources are for everybody. Religion, because religions are not philosophical systems that belong to man's genius; therefore, neither law, nor property or religion can be imposed on MAN; because these three annul and deprive him of his most precious RIGHTS: these are the assassins upon whom we have vowed to take our most boisterous revenge, these are the enemies upon whom we have declared a non stop war unto death."

"Of these three infamous enemies, **RELIGION** is the

one who must be the constant object of our deadly attacks because the people have never survived their religion; and **by killing Religion, LAW and PROPERTY will be at our mercy**; then, by establishing Masonic religion over the corpses of the three assassins, as well as Masonic law and Masonic property, we will be able to regenerate society."

"And since all our Masonic secrets are impenetrably hidden under symbols, those of the Supreme Degree to which you have arrived to are found hidden under the Symbol of Our Degree... you must do your part by maximizing the probability of good success, to the ends of immediately consecrating yourself effectively to the material realization of the double insignia:"

"DEUS MEUMQUE JUS."

(All rights for us)

"ORDO AB CHAO"

(Enemies of the order, liquidated)

While studying the double insignia to which a Mason consecrates himself, I discovered a document that was displayed in a gathering of 32nd and 33rd degrees which was called in Paris in October of 1885, by the very powerful sovereign Grand Commander of the Scottish Rite. It declared:

-"The Order demands to put into immediate practice the

"D:.M:.J:." Esoterically or overtly, D.M.J. are the initials of the 33rd degree insignia, Deus Meumque Jus, -God and my right-. Esoterically, in the secrecy of the Order, D:.M:.J:. are the initials of the words **Destruction, Materialization, Imposition**, which command to: Impose the Destruction of all that does not reach the Materialization." (A government based on material stimulus obviating the spiritual ones).

There was no letter "J" in the classical Latin alphabet. The word JUS, was actually IUS, spelled with an "I" before Medieval times, which is the reason why Free Masons have attached the secret word "Imposition," to "Jus," in their insignia.

The three periods (:.) seen in all Masonic works, which are characteristic in the personal signature of every Mason mean:

- **DESTRUCTION**
-Of the Supernaturalis, -of the Authority -of Anti-Freemasonry

- **MATERIALIZATION**
-Of the Conscience, -of The Teachings -of the State

- **IMPOSITION**
-Unto the Family, -Unto the Nation, -Unto Society

Relentless, subtle or shamelessly, the prince of darkness, Lucifer, has not ceased since the beginning of time to weave his net with the purpose of achieving a "world government." To this end, what better way to satisfy the spiritual thirst of man, than with rituals that distance him from the One True God. And, On the other end of the spectrum, to feed the worldly hunger of man, whose only god is himself, by offering him what he desires most: power and glory.

I have provided a brief account of the first and third degrees without having mentioned the second, as this degree is not as relevant by itself. However, it is the essence of the first three degrees in Freemasonry called the "Symbolic Degrees", which have the greatest importance. It's in these degrees, where the theoretical "purity" of Gnosticism is taught without beating around the bush. This philosophy is developed in greater detail in the "Rosicrucian" degree, to finally practice it in the 30th degree or "Knight Kadosh" (see Appendix 1).

Little by little, step-by-step, degree-by-degree, up the ascension ladder of the Freemasonry structure, its fundamental doctrine is patiently being sowed. As Zoroaster established, this doctrine consists of submitting all belief to human reasoning, to convert man into a being that is convinced he himself is god; a species of superman with the capacity, the right, and furthermore; with the duty to emit judgment over the destiny of humanity and to create the most grotesque philosophical theories.

How can one not shudder after discovering such a diabolically confused mindset, lost amongst deep darkness, capable of lifting up the great banner of its "faith", as the supreme "Truth." The mishmash, which makes up its dogma: A sum total of every pagan ritual added to the fantasies of ancient mythology; the most far-fetched legends and literary novels; the journeys created by Dante's runaway imagination, the deeds of Hercules and the adventures of Ulysses, of The Iliad and Virgil's The Odyssey.

How can one not feel a deep rejection and revulsion at an Organization that in order to boost man's ego, proclaims the great moral teaching by Pike in the 30th degree or of "Knight Kadosh"; "Me, and nothing more than me. Everything for me and this by any means necessary, whatever they may be."

The unwary soul that hopes to find the meaning of its existence by annihilating God and separating himself from Him; the soul that finds its vital reason for living in vanity and power, ends up lost in the labyrinth of darkness. Confused by obscurity, it feels rich, and lacking nothing, but as the Lord says in the book of Revelation, that soul is poor, miserable, blind, unfortunate and naked.

Where do these foundations of Freemasonry, so full of esotericism and mystery lead, with their rituals taken from the Order of Knights; who for many are fairytales, heroes and magicians, yet infected with satanic covenants and demons dressed as angels of light? What is the end purpose of these magical ceremonies, full of blood and crimes, hidden behind the falsely colored sky of an aberrant mysticism? It is a fanatical, mythic religion coated with the sweetening and narcotic powers of poetry, music and color.

It is where the most terrible books of ancient alchemy are foolishly awakened to chain the soul and blind the understanding. Containing ceremonies dedicated to having encounters with the afterlife, with the forbidden world of deceiving spirits, which open up as majestic and seductive doors, intoxicating the already captive spirit forever in the magic of the Knights Templar. They are rituals in which all proportion of logic and sensibility are lost, where the line between good and evil becomes a dense fog of shady concepts and of distorted symbols wherein the supposed Holy Grail (the cup from which Christ drank during the last supper) is transformed into a hallucinatory chalice of a covenant with Lucifer himself. They are worship services, where the souls, lost, blind and chained, fervently give themselves over to any fantasy overflowing with magical dreams of splendor, of power and of glory.

They are infernal gatherings in which the Cross of Calvary becomes the representation of the sexes that have united for the perpetual generation of everything that exists. The Knights of the Rosicrucian declare that God never created anything, but that all of creation comes from the universal generation, or, as Albert Pike's fearless audacity proclaims: "Everything originated in **Adonai, the bisexual god**". It is to this degree where all Christian mysteries are exposed to mockery and jeering, by the attendees to force the initiate to believe that Christianity is false, while the cross is constantly used in a blasphemous manner.

The seed is bred into the gullible and beginning Mason, so

that the hatred and destruction of everything that opposes its "noble doctrine," begin to take root.

"Afterwards, it bears fruit to the point to obtain the sublime right to kill and destroy everything that opposes the reigning of the universal generation in which Man will be the supreme King of the cosmos." (Secret instructions from the Great Sovereign Inspector Generals for the conduct of the lodges, chapters and councils by the Viscount of Jouquiere).

These are, without the false pretenses, the true aspirations to reach the great "superman" of Masonic doctrine. The Order exhorts its members to use reason, and it is also what I am asking you to do, beloved reader: Use reason and the fear of God.

CONCLUSION

A message for those that have been involved in Freemasonry

Since its origins, Freemasonry has been untiringly incubating the egg of its monstrous abomination, which today is on the verge of eclosion. Every Supreme Council is set in place. All its strategies have been established. The plan has been drawn up. The great hour is near. The moment so long awaited by the great heads of Freemasonry, the Grand Sovereign Instructors, is already near to reaching its most elevated expression. The Freemasons have in their hands, a most terrible weapon they have been building with great zeal.

All the pieces of their infamous puzzle are in their correct position: a workshop handles a portion of it and hundreds of workers, yet another, though almost all of them ignore the contribution they have made to the infernal ensemble. Regardless, all pieces adapt themselves perfectly one to another; all gears engage one to another; all parts relate and complement one to another: "The Weapon is created." The world economy is being unified.

The great majority of schools and universities have already been infiltrated by "New Age," which is the philosophical, humanistic and Gnostic thought that will be in charge of forming Superman within each person. "Masonic tolerance" invades the government structures; Tolerance to everything that offends God, as long as human rights are respected.

The oaths and covenants made with Lucifer by each initiate are indelible. Millions of Masons, millions of followers of the false christs and of the initiate doctrine, have remained contaminated in their spirit and bound to eternal condemnation. What will those glory filled great beings do, puffed up by the greatest titles that have never been attributed to any man: Sublime Knights, Princes of Jerusalem, Venerables, Sovereigns, Fathers of Truth, Omnipotents, as they are called in some rituals? Those who display themselves as relentless destroyers of the pure and holy message of Jesus Christ, what are they going to do before the "Great White Throne" when the papers of the great awards from the Lodges crumbles before the Book of Life where their names have not been inscribed?

It is by no vain gesture that Scripture mentions them in the Second Epistle of Timothy 3:1-8 where it says:

*"...There will be **terrible times** in the last days. People will be lovers of themselves, lovers of money, boastful, proud, abusive, disobedient to their parents, ungrateful, unholy, without love, unforgiving, slanderous, without self-control, brutal, not lovers of good, treacherous, rash, conceited, lovers of pleasure rather than lovers of God - having a form of godliness but denying its power. Have nothing to do with them. They are the kind who worm their way into homes and gain control over weak-willed women, who are loaded down with sins and are swayed by all kinds of evil desires, always learning but never able to acknowledge the truth. Just as Jannes and Jambres opposed Moses, so also these men oppose the truth - men of depraved minds, who, as far as the faith is concerned, are rejected."*   2 Timothy 3:1-8

All those who are involved, all those who have been initiated in Freemasonry's ranks, carry its mark on their heart; they have drunk from the chalice of the initiate, a chalice of magic from where the ancient Orders of Knighthood drank, and from which the Apprentice drinks in his initiation. The Bible cites a passage that should lead us to reflect:

*"Then I heard another voice from heaven say: "**Come out of her, my people**, so that you will not share in her sins, so that you will not receive any of her plagues; for her sins are piled up to heaven, and God has remembered*

her crimes. Give back to her as she has given; pay her back double for what she has done. Mix her a double portion from her own cup."   *Revelation 18:4-6*

I ask God's Holy Spirit that if this testimony has enlightened the eyes of your understanding, that it also grant you a deep repentance to come to the One who is the only one who frees you from the chains in which Satan has enslaved you to drag you to eternal condemnation. It is Jesus Christ, the Son of God, who said, "I am the Way, the Truth, and the Life. None comes to the Father but by Me." This way was opened through His own flesh, which was rent by our sins and through His blood that cleanses us from all evil. Only Jesus Christ can set you free and I am not talking about a religion, but about a personal relationship with the Spirit of Life, a real fellowship between your spirit and His. The true Temple of God is waiting for you. The only place, the Holy of Holies, where the presence of God can come and dwell... "A contrite and humble heart."

There are people of God involved in this Great Lie forged by the devil. There are even men and women who serve God in a church, deacons, priests and pastors who have allowed themselves to become wound up in this seductive lie from the "Angel of Light." Supposed servants of God, and I say supposed because one cannot serve two masters, either you will do well with one and poorly with the other or vice versa. God does not share His glory with anyone.

God does not regard as innocent, he who already knowing

His word and His name, becomes   part of Lucifer's ranks. Judge for yourself. God has left his will in writing for all men to read. Jesus said:

"I came not to judge the world, but to save the world...
the Word that I have spoken, the same shall judge him in
the Last Day".   *John 12:47-48*

Will God overlook the Great Abomination of Freemasonry? For you, it may be child's play to mingle with foreign gods, to believe in reincarnation and in astrology, or to invite spiritual beings to come in and inhabit your being through mind control; But what you may consider unimportant, may not be so to Lucifer and much less, to Jehovah.

God says with such clarity:

"You adulterous people, don't you know that friendship
with the world is enmity toward God? Anyone who chooses
to be a friend of the world becomes an enemy of God."
                                                    James 4:4

It is painful to see men and women who say they belong to God, trusting in Mason's favors more than in the God they claim to believe; seeking answers or for doors to open, by the power of Freemasonry and not through God's; seeking wisdom from the demonic Mysteries; proclaiming to be a profane one seeking Freemasonry's Light and thus denying the only true light who is Jesus Christ himself.

God is not a game, neither is His Truth something that can be mixed with the occult without spiritual consequences. He is Justice and Holiness. His mercy extends to all mankind through His Son, Jesus Christ, who the Father sent as the perfect and acceptable sacrifice for sin. All who accept Him, as their true Lord and Savior of their souls, shall be redeemed.

God wants to save you today. Perhaps you are fearful of the oaths you have made and by the terrible threats and curses that may come against you if you were to break these covenants. I want to tell you that Jesus loves you and He let himself be nailed to a cross, taking upon His body the curses that are over you.

It is written:

"The reason the Son of God appeared was to destroy the devil's work".   *1 John 3:8*

"Since the children have flesh and blood (this is in the physical nature of man), he too shared in their humanity so that by his death he might destroy him who holds the power of death - that is, the devil - and free those who all their lives were held in slavery by their fear of death."   *Hebrews 2:14-15*

The way to come to God is by invoking His Name. This is asking Him to enter and inhabit the temple of the Spirit, which is our inner being. Ask this with a repentant heart, with a sincere and firm decision to leave past sins, including

Freemasonry. God said:

"If my people, who are called by my name, will humble themselves and pray and seek my face and turn from their wicked ways, then will I hear from heaven and will forgive their sin and will heal their land."

2 Chronicles 7:14

The salvation of the soul is not just reciting a prayer, but consecrating one's life to God and living every day in His Truth. Jesus said:

"Behold, I am coming soon! My reward is with me, and I will give to everyone according to what he has done. I am the Alpha and the Omega, the First and the Last, the Beginning and the End. Blessed are those who wash their robes, that they may have the right to the tree of life and may go through the gates into the city. Outside are the dogs, those who practice magic arts, the sexually immoral, the murderers, the idolaters and everyone who loves and practices falsehood. I, Jesus, have sent my angel to give you this testimony for the churches. I am the Root and the Offspring of David, and the bright Morning Star".   *Revelation 22:12-17*

Those who have never been Masons are being affected by the curses of the Order

Unfortunately, not only those who are, or have been Masons are affected, but their children and their descendents as well.

After working with thousands of people that have come to us seeking deliverance, I realized how a great number of people are suffering from the consequences and curses that come from Freemasonry. Perhaps you, beloved reader, are an innocent victim among them. Please read the following list and if you find yourself among these cases, proceed to the following chapter and pray the prayer of renunciation found there.

1. If anyone in your ancestry was a Mason, you can be certain that you are under this influence paying a price that you shouldn't have to pay such as: Sickness, ruin, all kinds of misfortune of any kind, panic attacks and accidents, which are several consequences inherited from Freemasonry.

2. If you do not know the history of your ancestors, but there is someone among your siblings, cousins or uncles involved with this order, this is a clear indicator that somewhere in your ancestral line, there is involvement with Freemasonry. These close relatives felt attracted by this secret society because it was in their blood.

3. If you are, or have been under the spiritual authority of a pastor or priest that was a Mason, you have been the victim of the spiritual contamination coming from the occult spirits that are found in said authority.

4. If you are associated with a charitable institution associated with Freemasonry. Such as the Shriners, Lions club, Rotary club etc.

5. If you have sworn or signed documents approving Masonic decisions in politics or business.

6. If you are a member of a Knight Order, and they have done a ritual in order to vest you as a "Knight". Or if you have been vested with some spiritual gift through the "Knight" ritual, using swords (Many people get involved with this type of apparent social club, unaware of what is behind it).

7. If you belong or have belonged to clubs such as the "Boy Scouts". The oaths and rituals they conduct are Masonic.

8. If you, or one of your ancestors have been in the military and have been decorated. Many of these decorations are of Masonic origin.

9. If your last name has an emblem or a coat of arms. All of that symbolism comes from Freemasonry.

HOW TO BE FREE FROM FREEMASONRY AND ITS INFLUENCE

The covenants made in Freemasonry are serious and complex and their curses involve an entire generational blood line.

It is important to consciously break every one of them. You must do it with a deep repentance, and believe they are broken by the Blood of Jesus.

Here is a list, degree by degree, of all that has to be cancelled and broken. Even if you were only involved in the first degrees, I recommend you break all of them, because you declared that you were "one for all and all for one."

DELIVERANCE FROM FREEMASONRY

Allow me to lead you in exhaustive prayer to be set free from every covenant and curse coming from this Order.

One can only leave Freemasonry through the power of Jesus Christ. A life that has not first been consecrated to Him, will not find the desired freedom. Therefore, I suggest you first surrender your life to the Son of God. Recognize the sacrifice of the Cross as the only source of salvation and redemption for your sins. Repent deeply for your involvement in Freemasonry and all its sins. Finally, in your own words, invoke the Name of Jesus Christ, so that He may come and dwell in your heart. Once this is done, believe with all your heart and make a covenant with Him to follow and obey His Word with the help of the Holy Spirit. Seek the help of a Christian congregation to guide you in your New walk with Jesus.

PRAYER

-I renounce every position that I held in the Lodge, those of any of my ancestors or my own, including that of "Master", "Venerable Master" or any other. I renounce calling any man "master" because Jesus Christ is my only Master and Lord and He forbids anyone else to carry that title. I renounce causing others to fall into Freemasonry's trap and observing the hopelessness of others during the rites. I renounce the effects of Freemasonry that were transmitted from any of my female ancestors whose husband may have made her feel rejected and unworthy of trust, when he entered and attended a lodge and refused to tell her about their secret activities.

-I also renounce all obligations, curses and oaths enacted by all female members of my family through any direct membership with the Feminine Orders of Freemasonry, the Order of Eastern Star, or any other Masonic order or occult organization.

-In the name of our Lord Jesus Christ, I renounce and abandon all that involves me in Freemasonry and any other lodge, art, or occult practices on behalf of my ancestors and myself. I also renounce and break the code of silence imposed on me by Freemasonry and the Occult with my family.

-I renounce and I repent from all pride and arrogance that opened the doors for slavery and bondage to Freemasonry, which afflicts me and my family.

Apprentice 1'st Degree

-I renounce the first-degree covenant and the declaration of being in darkness and that the only light comes from Freemasonry.

-I renounce the rope around my neck and the curses upon my throat and my tongue. I renounce the fear of being trapped, claustrophobia and the spirits that produce asthma, hay fever, respiratory allergies, and respiratory illnesses.

-I renounce the serpent on the clasp of the apron, the spirit of python, which came to squeeze my spiritual life out of me. I renounce the ancient pagan teachings of Babylon and Egypt and the symbolism of the first tracing board. I renounce the mixture and fusion of truth and error, mythology, the fabrication of lies taught as truths and to falsehoods made by the leaders as the true comprehension of the rite, and to the blasphemy in this degree of Freemasonry.

-I renounce the Hoodwink or hooded darkness, the blindfold over my eyes and its effects upon my eyesight, emotions, fear of darkness, confusion, the fear of light and sudden noises.

-I renounce the sweet drink and the bitter drink and I cancel the curse of bitterness upon my life, and the curse of the Great Architect of the Universe for leaving Freemasonry.

-I renounce the secret word "Boaz" and all that it means, to every curse and sickness over the uterus.

-I renounce the tip of the compass, the sword or spear held at my chest, the fear of death and the fear of being stabbed, and heart attacks.

-I renounce and sever every tie and protection from the element spirits (fire, water, air and earth).

-I renounce the symbols of Freemasonry and their power over my life and that of my descendants: the square, the compass, the hammer, the level, the chisel, the ruler, the pentagram, the hexagram, the octagon, (stars of 5, 6 and 8 points) and the star of twelve points. I renounce the covering of the apron, the flaming sword and to all the symbols of duality.

-I renounce the Great Architect of the Universe with all his names.

-I renounce the absolute confidentiality demanded under an oath of witchcraft and sealed by kissing the volume of the sacred law.

-I loose my destiny that was bound to the unhewn rock and to the polished rock.

-I command all captivity in which my soul has been trapped in the three regions of hell to be destroyed. I command my soul to be set free.

-I break the covenant of unity that I made with all Masonic brotherhood.

-I break the covenant signed with my blood in which I became a member of the order.

-I renounce every curse and every infirmity in my blood. I declare a Jesus Christ blood transfusion in my veins, cleansing my blood.

-I renounce the pride of a confirmed character and the good prestige demanded to join Franc masonry and the proper consequential self-judgment of being good enough to go before God without the need of a Savior.

-I put my throat, vocal chords and respiratory system under the absolute government of Jesus Christ.

-I renounce the power of all Masonic symbols. I decree that its influence will not touch my life or that of my family.

2nd Degree "Companion"

-In the name of Jesus, I renounce the oaths and curses involved in the second degree or skilled communion of Freemasonry, especially the curses upon the heart and chest.

-I renounce the secret words SHIBOLET and JACIN and all that they mean. I renounce the ancient pagan teaching and symbolism of the second tribunal of investigation.

-I renounce the sign of reverence at the generative principle.

-I renounce all magic geometry and the spirit of Plato and Pythagoras.

-I cut emotional insensitivity, apathy, indifference, unbelief and deep wrath in me and in my family, in the name of Jesus Christ.

-I pray for healing in the chest, lungs, the area of the heart and also for the healing of my emotions and I ask to become sensitive to the Holy Spirit of God.

3rd Degree "Master"

-I renounce, in the name of Jesus, oaths taken and curses involved in the third degree or master degree of Freemasonry, especially the curses upon the stomach and abdominal area. I renounce the secret words MAHA BONE (HESO DE MAHA) TUBAL CAIN and MACHABEN, MACHBINNA and everything they mean.

-I renounce the ancient teaching and symbolism of the third tribunal of investigation used in the ritual. I renounce the spirit of death represented as the rituals of murder, fear of death, false martyrdom, being afraid of violent gang attack, assault or rape, and the impotence of this degree.

-I renounce the death covenant I made by getting into the coffin or lying on the stretcher involved in the death ritual.

-I command my soul to leave all captivity of death allowed through this ceremony.

-I renounce the spirit of Hiram Abiff, the false savior of the Masons, revealed in this degree.

-I renounce the false resurrection.

-In the name of Jesus, I pray for the healing of the stomach, bladder, belly, liver and any other body organ affected by Freemasonry and I ask for God's mercy and understanding to be loosed over me and my family.

-I renounce the pagan ritual of the "Point inside a circle" with all its bondages and phallic worship. I renounce the <<G>> symbol with its symbolism and occult pagan ties. I renounce occult mysticism from the black and white tiles with the mosaic borders and the gleaming five-pointed star.

-I renounce the all-seeing eye, the third eye or Horus' forehead eye and its pagan and occult symbolism. I now close that third eye and all its occult ability to see inside the spiritual kingdom, in the name of the Lord Jesus Christ, and I put my trust in the Holy Spirit for all I need to know about spiritual matters.

-I renounce all false communions taken, all mockery of the redemptive work of Jesus Christ on the cross of Calvary, all unbelief, confusion and depression.

-I renounce and abandon every lie from Freemasonry that man is not a sinner, but simply imperfect, and that he can redeem himself through good works.

-I renounce all fear of madness, anguish, death wishes, suicide and death in the name of Jesus Christ.

-I renounce all wrath, hatred, thoughts of murder, vengeance, reprisals, spiritual apathy, false religions, all unbelief, especially towards the Holy Bible as the Word of God and all patronizing the Word of God.

-I renounce all spiritual seeking within false religions.

-I renounce initiative death and the spirit of death.

- Now command the spirit of death to leave your life in the name of Jesus Christ. Put your hands on your head, then on the nape of your neck and then on your forehead, and say:

-I close every spiritual door that was opened in this ceremony, by me or by my ancestors.

-I declare healing upon my stomach, my gall bladder, and intestines, liver and throughout my entire digestive system, in the name of Jesus Christ.

Chapter Degrees

-I renounce and abandon the oaths and curse involved in the "York Ritual" of Freemasonry.

-I renounce the mark of the Lodge, and the mark in the form of squares and the angels assigned to a person for life.

-I also reject and renounce the jewel or occult talisman that was made with this sign that is used in Lodge meetings;

I renounce the degree of master marked with his secret word JOPPA, and its punishment of having the right ear tormented and the curse of permanent deafness, as well as having my right hand severed for being an imposter.

-I renounce and abandon the oaths made and the curses involved in the other degrees of the "York Rite", among them that of "master of the past," with the punishment that my tongue would be cut in half from its root.

-I renounce the degree of "most excellent master," whose punishment is that my chest would be opened, my vital organs pulled out and that they would be displayed until they rotted on the dunghill.

-I renounce the titles, with their oaths and curses of all chapter degrees of incarnate Freemasonry that are:

Degree 4: "Secret Master"

-I renounce the oaths made and to the curses and the punishments involved in the United States and the Lodges of the Orient, including the degree of Secret Master, its secret password ADONAI and its punishments.

Degree 5: "Perfect Master"

-I renounce the degree of Perfect Master, its secret password MHAHAH-BONE, and its punishment of being struck against the ground during an attack.

Degree 6: "Intimate Secretary"

-I renounce the degree of Intimate Secretary, to its password JEHOVAH, used in a blasphemous fashion and its punishment that they would dissect my body and cut my vital organs in pieces and throw them to the beasts of the field.

Degree 7: "Prevost" or "Rector" and "Judge"

-I renounce the degree of Rector and Judge, and to its secret password HIRUMTITO-CIVI-KY, and the punishment that my nose be cut off.

Degree 8: "Quartermaster of Buildings"

-I renounce the degree of Builder, and to its secret password AKAR-JAI-JAH, and to the punishment that they would pluck out my eyes, cut my body in two and leave my intestines exposed.

Degree 9: "Elected Master of Nine"

-I renounce the degree of Elected Knight of Nine, its secret password NEKAM NAKAH, and its punishment that they cut off my head and hang me from the highest post in the Orient.

Degree 10: "Elected Master of Fifteen"

-I renounce the Fifteenth Degree of Illustrious Elected, to its secret password ELIGNAM and to its punishment of opening my body perpendicularly and horizontally with my entrails exposed to the air for eight hours so the flies can attack it, in addition to cutting off my head and placing it on a high peak.

Degree 11: "Sublime Elected Knight"

-I renounce the degree of Sublime Elected Knight of Twelve, and its secret password STOLKIN-ADONAI, and its punishment of cutting my hands in two.

Degree 12: "Great Master Architect"

I renounce the degree of Great Master and Architect, and its secret password RAB-BANAIM and its punishments.

Degree 13: "Great Master of the Royal Holy Arch"

-I renounce the degree of the Knight of the Ninth Arch of Solomon and its secret password JEHOVAH, and its punishment of giving my body up as prey to the beasts of the forest and that my brain be exposed to the burning sun.

-I renounce the false secret name of God, JAHBULON, and I declare a total rejection of the worship to false pagan gods, Bul or Baal and On or Osiris and the counterfeit Jah. I also renounce the password AMMI RUJAMA and all that it means.

-I renounce the false communion or Eucharist made in this degree, and to every mockery, skepticism and unbelief about the redeeming work of Jesus Christ on the Cross of Calvary. I cut all its curses and their effects upon my life and that of my family in the name of Jesus Christ, and I pray for healing of the mind, the brain, etc.

-I renounce and abandon the oaths and curses involved in this degree of Royal Master of the York Rite, the degree of Select Master with its punishments that they cut my hands to the stump, pluck my eyes from their sockets and chop my body into quarters and throw it into the garbage of the temple.

-I renounce and abandon all the oaths and curses involved in the degree of Super Excellent Master, together with the punishment that they cut off my thumbs, pluck out my eyes and tie up my body with chains and shackles, and that they take me captive to a strange land.

-I renounce the Order of the Knights of the Red Cross, together with the punishment that my house would be torn down and my body hung from its beams.

-I renounce the degree of Knights Templar and the secret password KEB RAIOTH and also the degree of Knight of Malta and its secret password MAHER-SHALAL-HASH-BAZ.

-I renounce the vows made over the human skull, the crossed swords and the curse of Judas' death wish for my head to be cut off and placed on the steeple of a church.

-I renounce the ungodly communion and especially drinking from a human skull in many rites.

Continuation of Chapter Degrees

Renounce the titles, pacts and the curses of the following degrees:

Degree 14: "Great Elect, Perfect Mason or Mason of the Sublime Sacred Vault"

-I renounce the degree of Great Elect, Perfect and Sublime Mason, its secret password and to its punishment that my body be opened and my intestines removed as food for the vultures.

COUNCIL OF PRINCES OF JERUSALEM

Degree 15: "Knight of the Orient or of the Sword"

-I renounce the degree of Knight of the Orient, and its secret password RAPH-O-DOM, and to its punishments.

Degree 16: "Prince of Jerusalem"

-I renounce the degree of Prince of Jerusalem, its secret password TEBET-ADAR and its punishment of being made naked and to having my heart pierced with a ritual dagger.

Degree 17: "Knight of the Orient"

Degree 18: "Sovereign Prince, Rosicrucian or Rose Cross Knight"

-I renounce the covenants taken and the curses made with the most Wise Supreme Knight Pelican and of the Eagle and the Sovereign Prince Rose Cross of Heredom.

-I renounce all Rosicrucian witchcraft and Kabbalah.

-I renounce the expression that the death of Jesus Christ was a "Horrendous Calamity" and the deliberate mockery of the Christian doctrine of atonement.

-I renounce the blasphemy against Jesus Christ and the secret words IGNE, NATURA, RENOVATUR, INTEGRA.

-I renounce the mockery of communion made in this degree.

PHILOSOPHICAL DEGREES OR KADOSH DEGREES (BLACK FREEMASONRY)
Council of Kadosh

Degree 19: "Great Pontiff of the Heavenly Jerusalem or Sublime Scotsman"

-I renounce the oaths made and the curses and the punishments involved in the degree of Great Pontiff, its secret password EMMANUEL and its punishments.

Degree 20: "Venerable Grand Master of the Symbolic Lodges, Master ad Vitam"

-I renounce the oaths of the degree of Grand Master of the Symbolic Lodges, and its secret passwords JEKSON and STOLKIN, and its punishments.

Degree 21: "Prussian Knight or Noachite Patriarch"

-I renounce the covenants and oaths of the degree of Noachite Knight of Prussia, its secret password PELEG and its punishments.

Degree 22: "Prince of Lebanon (Libanus) or Knight of the Royal Arch"

-I renounce the covenants and oaths of the degree of Knight of the Royal Arch, and its secret password NOEBEZALEEL-SODONIAS and its punishments.

Degree 23: "Chief of the Tabernacle"

-I renounce the covenants and oaths of the degree of Chief of the Tabernacle, its secret password URIELJEHOVA, and its punishment that I came into agreement for the earth to open and swallow me to the neck until I die.
19 Grand Pontiff
20 Master ad Vitam

21 Patriarch Noachite

22 Prince of Libanus

23 Chief of the Tabernacle

24 Prince of The Tabernacle

25 Knight of the Brazen Serpent

26 Prince of Mercy

27 Commander of the Temple

28 Knight of the Sun

29 Knight of St. Andrew

30 Grand Elect Knight Kadosh

31 Grand Inspector Inquisitor Commander

32 Sublime Prince of The Royal Secret

Degree 24: "Prince of the Tabernacle"

-I renounce the covenants and oaths of the degree of Prince of the Tabernacle, and its punishment that I should be stoned to death and that my body should remain unburied as it rots.

Degree 25: "Knight of the Brazen Serpent"

-I renounce the covenants and oaths of the degree of Knight of the Bronze Serpent, to its secret password MOSES-JOHANNES and its punishment that poisonous serpents should eat my heart.

Degree 26: "Prince of Grace or of the Mercy or Scottish Trinitarian"

-I renounce the covenants and oaths of the degree of Prince of Mercy, its secret password GOMEL, JEHOVA-JACHIN, and its punishment of condemnation and evil throughout the universe.

Degree 27: "Great Commander of the Temple"

-I renounce the covenants and oaths of the degree of Knight Commander of the Temple, its secret password SOLOMON, and its punishment of Almighty God's most severe anger being inflicted upon me.

Degree 28: "Knight of the Sun"

-I renounce the covenants and oaths of the degree of Knight Commander of the Sun, or degree of Prince Adept, its secret password STIBIUM, and its punishments of searing my tongue with a red hot iron, ripping my eyes out, removing my sense of smell and hearing, cutting off my hands, and being left for voracious animals to destroy me or to be executed by lightning from heaven.

Degree 29: "Great Scott or Knight of Saint Andrew"

-I renounce the covenants and oaths of the degree to Scottish Knight of Saint Andrews, its secret password NEKAMA-EURLAC, and its punishments.

Degree 30: "Great Pontiff of the Kadosh Council or of the Black and White Eagle" also "Great Elect Knight Kadosh

-I renounce the covenants and oaths from the degree of Great Pontiff of the Council of Kadosh, its secret password EMMANUEL and its punishments.

SUBLIME DEGREES

Degree 31: "Great Inspector Inquisitor Commander"

-I renounce the covenants and oaths made and to the curses involved in degree 31 of Freemasonry, the Great Knight of Kadosh and Knight of the Black and White Eagle. I renounce the secret password STIBIUM ALCABAR, PHARASH-KOH and all that they mean.

-I renounce all gods and goddesses of Egypt that are honored in this degree, including Anubis with its Jackal head. Osiris the sun god, Isis, the sister and wife of Osiris and also the goddess of the moon.

-I renounce the Soul of Queres, the false symbol of immortality, the Death chamber and the false teaching of reincarnation.

-I renounce Lucifer and his doctrine.

Degree 32: "Sublime and Valiant Prince of the Royal Secret"

I renounce the covenants and oaths of this degree as well as its curses and punishments: the Sublime Prince of the Royal Secret. I renounce the secret password FAAL/FARASH-KOL and all that they mean. I renounce the false Masonic Trinitarian deity, AUM, and its parts: Brahma, the creator, Vishnu, the preserver, and Shiva, the destroyer. I renounce the deity of AHURA-MAZDA, the solicited or fountain spirit of all light. I renounce worshipping with fire, which is an abomination to God, and also from drinking from a human skull as inacted in many rituals.

Degree 33 and Supreme Degree

In the name of Jesus, I renounce the oaths made and the curses involved in the thirty-third degree of Franc masonry and of the Great Sovereign Inspector General. I renounce its secret passwords, DEMOLAY-HIRUM ABIFF, FREDERICK OF PRUSSIA, MICHA, MACHA, BEALIM and ADONAI and everything that they mean. I renounce all the duties in every Masonic degree and all the punishments invoked.

-I renounce and completely abandon the Great Architect of the Universe, who in this degree reveals himself as Lucifer, and his false declaration of having God's universal paternity. I renounce the priestly collar. I renounce the skeleton whose cold arms are invited if the oath of this degree is violated and I renounce its poison.

-I renounce the rope noose around my neck.

-I renounce the infamous assassins of their grand master, their law, their property, and their religion. I renounce the greed and witchcraft involved in the attempt to manipulate and dominate the rest of humanity.

-In the name of God the Father, Jesus Christ His Son, and the Holy Spirit, I renounce all of the above and to the curses involved with idolatry, blasphemy, confidentiality and the deceit of Freemasonry at every level. I appropriate the blood of Jesus to cleanse its consequences from my life. I now rebuke all prior consent given by any one of my ancestors and by myself to be deceived.

ALL OTHER DEGREES

-I renounce the rest of the oaths made, the rituals of any other degree and the curses involved, which include the degrees of Allies, Red Cross of Constantine, the Order of the Secret Listener and the Royal Masonic Order of Scotland.

-I renounce the other lodges and secret societies including the Freemasonry of Prince Hall, the Lodges of the Great Orient, Mormonism, the Order of Amaranth, The Royal Order of Jesters, The Order of the Fraternity of Unity of Manchester, Buffalos, Druids, Arboleros, Loyal Orange, the Black and Purple Lodges, the Moose, Elk and Eagle Lodges, the Ku Klux Klan, the Grange, the Tree Fellers of the World, the Riders of the Red Robe, the Knights of Pythia and the Mystic Order of the Veiled Prophets of the Enchanted Realm. I renounce the Women's Order of the Eastern Star, the Daughters of the Eastern Star, the International Order of Job's Daughters, The Internationa Order of the Rainbow for Girls, The Order of the Children of De Molay and its effects on myself and my entire family.

Lord Jesus, because I want to be totally free from all of these occult ties, I will burn or destroy all objects in my possession that connect me to any lodge or occult organization, including Freemasonry, witchcraft and Mormonism, and any charm, apron, book of rituals, rings and any jewelry. I renounce the effects of these and other objects of Freemasonry, including the compass and the square that I or my family may have had, in the name of our Lord Jesus Christ.

-I renounce all unclean spirits associated with Freemasonry, witchcraft and any other sin. I command in the name of our Lord Jesus Christ, that satan and all his spirits be bound and cast out of me now, without touching or hurting anyone, and going to the place assigned to them by our Lord Jesus to never return to me or my family. I seek the name of our Lord Jesus Christ to set us free of these spirits, according to the many promises of the Bible. I ask to be delivered of any spirit of infirmity, curse, affliction, addiction, evil or allergy associated with these sins that I have now confessed and renounced.

Shriners (Applies only to the United States)

-I renounce the oaths, deeds, curses and punishments involved in the Ancient Arabian Order of the Nobles of the Mystic Sanctuary. I renounce the piercing of my eyeballs with a three-edged blade, the removal of the flesh from my feet, madness and the worship of the false god Allah as the god of our fathers. I renounce deceit, the practice of hanging, decapitation, drinking the victim's blood, being urinated on by dogs during the initiation and the offering of urine as a commemoration.

FINAL POINTS IN THE DELIVERANCE SESSION

It is necessary to carry out the following actions in faith:

1. Symbolically remove the blindfold from your eyes, (which represents deceit), and decree that it is burned with fire.

2. Symbolically remove the veil of mourning.

3. Symbolically cut and remove the rope from your neck and the mark it left. Decree that they are burned with fire.

4. Renounce the false Masonic pact of matrimony. Remove the ring of this false wedding from the fourth finger of your right hand and decree that it is burned with fire.

5. Symbolically remove the chains and bondages of

Freemasonry from your body.

6. Symbolically remove all Masonic clothing and armor, especially the apron.

7. Symbolically remove the ankle bracelets, chains and shackles.

8. Remove the swords which cover you above your head.

9. Symbolically get out of the coffin and decree that you leave the region of death where you were held captive.

10. If your own name is associated with the name of some deity or with an ancestor that was in Freemasonry, renounce your name and ask God for a new name. Write the old name on a piece of paper and burn it, in the name of Jesus.

11. All family coats of arms are associated with Freemasonry. Obtain the shield representing your family, burn it and decree that every Masonic pact is broken over the last name of your household.

CONCLUDING PRAYER

Holy Spirit, I ask you to show me anything else that I must do or for which I should pray, for my family and myself to be totally free from the consequences of the sins of Freemasonry, witchcraft, Mormonism and all paganism and its related occultism.

Pause at this point while you listen to God and pray because the Holy Spirit will lead you.

Now, beloved Father God, I humbly ask that by the blood of Jesus, Your Son and my Savior, cleanse me from all these sins that I have confessed and renounced and that you cleanse my spirit, soul, mind, emotions and every part of my body that has been affected by these covenants and curses in the name of Jesus Christ. I also command that every cell of my body now enter into divine order and be healed and whole as designed by our beloved Creator, including the restoration of my spirit, any chemical imbalance, neurological malfunctions controlling all carcinogenic cells and reversing all degenerative illnesses, in the name of the Lord Jesus.

I ask you Lord Jesus, that you baptize me now in your Holy Spirit, according to the promises of your Word. I rejoice in your protection and your power. Help me to walk in your righteousness and never go back. I enthrone you, Jesus Christ, in my heart because you are my Lord and Savior, the fountain of life. Thank you, Father God, for your mercy, your forgiveness and your love, in the name of Jesus the Son of the living God. Amen.

As a follow up for complete deliverance and to truly see the power of God manifest in your lives, I recommend you read my books: Iniquity, Eat My Body and Drink My Blood and Regions of Captivity. These books contain deep revelation about the spiritual world that will change your lives dramatically.

APPENDIX

The rite of the Order of KNIGHTS BENEFICENT OF THE HOLY CITY is manifested in three periods: The first before David, the second in 1118 and the third in 1313. In 1782 it joined the Great Orient of France.

Even when the accepted date of the foundation for the first lodges is 1641, tangible proofs are registered in 1655 to 1670.

The rite of the ANCIENT, FREE AND ACCEPTED MASONS OF ENGLAND was founded in 1717. This rite comprised seven degrees and functioned by giving to every man of good reputation the possibility of initiation.

In 1720, Juan de Toland inaugurated the SOCRATIC RITE that was a secret association of pantheists.

In 1721, SWEDENBORG's system came to put a mystical value to Toland's foundation. This Freemasonry had eight degrees, the last of which "Kadosh" was conferred according to convenience, more towards the elements of spiritual realization than to "masters in kabbalah".

The Baron of Ramsay created a Franc Masonry in France in 1728, that bore his name and that functioned with three degrees, the last of which had the title of Knight of the Temple.

THE RITE OF THE IRISH CHAPTER was established in 1730. That same year in 1730, FREEMASONRY OF ADOPTION was inaugurated and was not recognized by the Great East of France until 1774.

In 1739, in Silesia a religious order of Franc Masonry called RITE OF THE CONGREGATION OF THE MORAVIAN BROTHERHOOD is formed.

THE RITE OF THE ILLUMINATI or ILLUMINATED is manifested in 1745 according to the manual of Swedenborg.

In 1747, E. Estuard founds in Arras (France) the PRIMORDIAL CHAPTER OF THE ROSICROSSE.

In 1758, the FREEMASONRY OF HEREDON is founded in Paris or better said of PERFECTION with twenty-five degrees;

it is the first time the higher degrees appear.

THE PRIMITIVE SCOTTISH RITE presents three categories: the first in Paris, in 1758, made up of twenty-five degrees of initiation; the second is founded in Narbonne (France) with only ten degrees, and the third in Namur (Belgium), but thirty-three degrees do not appear until 1818.

THE MODERN FRENCH RITE makes its appearance in Paris, in 1761. It was founded in 1772 and proclaimed in 1773 by the Great Orient of France under the direction of the Grand Master of French Freemasonry, Felipe de Orleans, Duke of Chartres. In 1774, eager to find a formula that would harmonize the different heterogenous doctrines disseminated over a motley of degrees, the Great Orient charged a commission of the most distinguished Masons among whom were Bacon de la Chevalerie, Count of Stroganof, Baron of Toussaint and others, to conduct a detailed study and review of all known systems in order to formulate a new rite composed by the smallest number of degrees possible.

However, this commission, upon seeing the size of the issue at hand, resigned to the task and proposed to the Great Orient the suppression of the highest degrees. This was accepted by the Great Orient, who decided to recognize only the three degrees of initiation of symbolism. But later they again accepted the seven original degrees, which are:

Blue and Symbolic Degrees: 1. Apprentice; 2. Companion; 3. Master;

Superior Degrees: 4. Elected; 5. Scottish; 6. Knight of he Orient 7. RosiCrosse.

In 1766, in Marbourg, the reformed RosiCrosse take up the name SCHROEDER FREEMASONRY, and seriously practice magic and alchemy.

In this same year, Baron Tschoudy founds in Paris the Rite of the ORDER OF THE FLAMING STAR, with ten degrees.

THE RITE OF THE INITIATION OF PRIESTS is formed in 1767, in Berlin, with seven degrees, of which the final one is that of prophet or SAPHENATH PANCAH.

In 1771, Adam Weishaupt founds the RITE OF THE ILLUMINATED ONES OF BAVIERA, with thirteen degrees, that last of which is Man King.

In 1774, Bruneteau founds the PHILOSOPHIC SCOTTISH RITE, from the mother lodge of France.

In 1776, Boileau copies the Hermetic initiation of Montpelier and forms in Paris a group that he calls PHILOSOPHIC SCOTTISH RITE; besides encompassing the three traditional base degrees, he adds the ten following degrees:

4. Knight of the Sun
5. Knight of Phoenix
6. Sublime Philosopher
7. Knight of Iris

8. True Mason
9. Knight of Argonaut
10. Knight of the Golden Fleece
11. Initiated Perfect Great Inspector
12. Great Inspector or Great Scotsman
13. Sublime Master of the Luminous Ring

In 1777, the Jesuits of Scotland conceive the idea of imitating Franc Masonry and group them under the name of Royal Arch (better known as the RITE OF YORK, the place where the headquarters of the Masons of England were located). This rite is composed of four degrees, a number that dominates its regimen and which are the vows of the Company of Jesus.

These degrees are: 1. Past Master; 3. Super Excellent Mason and 4. Holy Royal Arch.

In America, this rite is composed of the following nine degrees: 1. Apprentice; 2. Companion; 3. Master; 4. Past Master; 5. Mark Master; 6. Very Excellent Master; 7. Royal Arch; 8. Royal Master; 9. Elected Master.

In 1779, Jose Balsamo, called Cagliostro, founds his famous EGYPTIAN RITE, that was a kind of Freemasonry of Adoption, with three fundamental degrees, where it attempted overall to follow not only the initiations according to the knowledge of the priests of the pyramids, but also to profess magic, astrology, etc.

In 1780, a Lodge of the RITE OF THE PHILADELPHES OF NARBONNE opens. In its origin, this rite was made up of six degrees, the last of which was the Prince of Jerusalem. Then four more were added, ending with the title of Rose Cross of the Great Rosary.

In 1782, the rite of GRAND CHAPTER GENERAL OF FRANCE is formed. In 1782, the RITE OF STRICT OBSERVANCE disappears from the public that had been born with Pedro de Aumont. Aside from the Order of Christ, that is the regrouping of the emigrated Templar Knights, Strict Observance is the only institution that maintained some relationship with the celebrated knighthood. The Order of Strict Observance ends up being up to a point, the model of the fraternal institution because the Order of Christ is more the reconstitution of part of the Templar Knights, but in its religious aspect; whereas the Strict Observance was more so in its esoteric dogma. After its dissolution, thanks to some elements who continued meeting in secret groups, that part of the templar institution has remained intact.

Towards the end of 1786, the famous ANCIENT AND ACCEPTED SCOTTISH RITE appears in France that was later formed in Scotland in 1846. This branch of Freemasonry has become very important, because of its being the most exoteric, that is to say, the one that opens its doors most easily to the profane world. It is so popular among neophytes that it not only represents a rite but the entire Freemasonry. The bulk of the public does not ignore it and its thirty-three degrees have become common language.

The thirty-three degrees are as follows:

SYMBOLIC DEGREES (Blue Freemasonry)
- Apprentice
- Companion
- Master

CHAPTER DEGREES (Freemasonry Incarnated)
- Secret Master
- Perfect Master
- Intimate Secretary
- Prevost and Judge
- Quartermaster of Buildings
- Master Elect of Nine
- Master Elect of Fifteen
- Sublime Knight Elect
- Grand Master Architect
- Grand Master of the Royal Arch
- Grand Elect Perfect or Sublime Mason of the Sacred Vault
- Knight of the Orient or of the Sword
- Prince of Jerusalem
- Knight of East and of West
- Sovereign Prince, Rose Cross or Knight Rose Cross

PHILOSOPHICAL DEGREES (Black Freemasonry)
- Grand Pontiff of Heavenly Jerusalem or Sublime Scotsman
- Venerable Grand Master of the Regular Lodge
- Prussian Knight or Noachite Patriarch

- Prince of Lebanon or Knight of the Royal Arch
- Superintendent of the Tabernacle
- Prince of the Tabernacle
- Knight of the Bronze Serpent
- Prince of Grace or Scottish Trinitarian
- Grand Commander of the Temple
- Knight of the Sun
- Grand Scottish Knight of Saint Andrew
- Grand Elect Kadosh Knight or Knight of the Black and White Eagle

SUBLIME DEGREES (White Freemasonry)
- Grand Inspector Inquisitor Commander
- Sublime and Brave Prince of the Royal Secret
- Sovereign Grand Inspector General

In 1801, Cuvalier de Trie founded THE SACRED ORDER OF THE SOPHISTICATES, whose third and final degree is Member of the Grand Ministers.

It is in Italy where in 1805, the EGYPTIAN OR JUDAIC RITE appears, better known as MISRAIM.

The Misraim Rite has ninety symbolic degrees: degrees 1 through 33 are philosophical; 34 through 36 mystical, 66 through 67 hermetic; and 78 through 90. This rite offers an extensive scale of initiation in order to delineate the categories of individuals. It preserves a symbolism in the teachings which is quite esteemed because it is closer to Ancient Ministries than the other rites. Its ritualistic system is well presented, especially when it comes to esoteric values.

The rite of the ORDER OF THE TEMPLE, that had given birth to the Order of Strict Observance during its era of hidden existence, only manifests in April of 1808. In 1816, some of Napoleon's companions had joined the Freemasonry under the name of RITE OF FRENCH NOACHITES. In 1839, Marconi and Moutet, in France, activate the old Rite of the East named Memphis with its 97 degrees. Aside from the rites we have listed, it is necessary to add the ALEXANDRIAN RITE that was especially formed to respect the basis teaching of astronomy; it is sometimes referred to as ISIAC RITE due to the worship of the phallus that was practiced there related to the mysteries of Isis. It's really not possible in the limited space of this small book to refer to the legend of Horus and all Osirian mythology.

Briefly, we will name the ANCIENT REFORMED RITE, a variant of the French model, practiced in Belgium and Holland; the RITE OF THE LIONS, mainly based on the teaching of Zoroastro and the practice of astrology. We should also add the MEXICAN NATIONAL RITE, that functions with 33 degrees, being the final one the Grand Inspector General of the Order; the ORFICO RITE.

REINCARNATION

I want to briefly touch on the topic of reincarnation, since many people have had experiences in which they assure they have lived during other times.

A friend of mine that was involved with esoteric philosophy had a revelation about this from God's Holy Spirit.

HERTA'S TESTIMONY

"Back then when I was heading down that path, I believed in reincarnation. When I began to walk with the Lord Jesus Christ and learned His word says that man dies once and after this comes judgment, I asked Him in what manner could I teach people who believed in reincarnation that it was not true.

One day, while washing dishes in my house, the Holy Spirit talked to me and said, "Look, the spirit of man is eternal, therefore the unclean spirits are as well. When a man dies, his spirit returns to God who gave it. The unclean spirit needs a physical body to inhabit and manifest itself.

The Word says that when it leaves the man (whether due to death or deliverance) it wanders, seeking a place to inhabit. Then, what happens is that these unclean spirits have known different people during many ages, so they come and tell the person they now inhabit that they've had past lives, pointing out names, places and situations. The devil is a liar and reincarnation is one of his great falsehoods."

Reincarnation is a process of spiritual purification through which man climbs a spiritual ladder from life to life, as the oriental philosophers affirm. If this were true, it is logical that today we would be living in a sublime world. But reality seems to indicate the contrary. The world has never been so full of vice and as corrupt as it is today. There has never been as much wickedness or violence, while the moral values are being lost day after day.

BIBLIOGRAPHY

- The Bible, New International Version 1960.
  Inspired by God, written by over 40 authors

- El libro negro de la francmasonería (The Black book of Francmasonry)
  De la Ferriere Serge Raynaud, 4 Ed. Diana, Editorial Menorah, 1985, pp.139.

- Manual del Aprendiz (Learning Manual)
  Lavagnini, Aldo 7ª Ed., Editorial. Kier, Bs. As.170 pp.

- El Simbolismo Hermenético (Hermetic Symbolism)
  Oswald Wirth

- LITURGY OF THE ANCIENT AND ACCEPTED SCOTTISH RITE, PART II, III, IV.

- The Kybalion
  A Study of the Hermetic philosophy of Ancient Egypt and Greece by Three Initiates. The Yogi Publication Society Masonic Temple, Chicago, IL 1912. pg 67.

- The Silva Method in order to obtain help from the other side
  Silva, Jose and Stone. Robert B. Pocket Books First Pocket Printer 1978 New York U.S.A. pg. 223

- Alquimia (Alchemy)
  Burckhardt, Titus. Paidos Iberica Ediciones S A, 1994, pp. 200.

- Símbolos fundamentales de la Ciencia Sagrada (Fundamental Symbols of Sacred Science)
  Guénon, René. Sophia Perennis, 2 Edition, 2004, pp. 476.

- Masoneria. Símbolos y Ritos. (Masonry Symbols and Rites)
  Ariza, Francisco. Editorial Symbolos, Barcelona 2002. pp. 224.

- Enigmas de la Historia (Secrets of History)
  De la Cierva Ricardo. Editor Fenix, 2003, pp. 264.

- La Vida Oculta de la Masonería (The Occult Life of Masonry)
  Leadbeater C.W. Berbera Editores, 2005, pp. 288.

- A los Pies del Maestro (At the Feet of the Master)
  Krishnamurti, J. 1 Ed. 22 Reimp, Bs. Aires, 2007, Kier.

- The Secret Doctrine
  Blavatsky, Helena, the Theosophical Publishing Company Limited, London, 1888. pg. 675.

- The Book Of The Master Of Hidden Places
  Adams, Marsham W. Kessinger Publishing, 2003 pg. 236.

- The Arcana Of Freemasonry
  Churchward, Albert. Cosimo Inc, 2007, pg. 326.

- Diary Of A Freemason
  Vaughan, David. Sovereign World, Chichester, England pg.198.

- The Book Of Dead
  Budge, E. A. Wallis. The book of the Dead. The chapters of coming forth by day, Volume 1. Londres, 1898.

- Anti-Masonry
  Oxford English Dictionary (Compact Edition), Oxford University Press, 1979, pg. 369.

- The New World Order
  Robertson, Pat Thomas Nelson. 1992, pg. 336.

- Proofs Of A Conspiracy
  Robinson, John. 4 Ed. New York,1798, pg. 134.

- Lost Keys Of Freemasonry
  Hall, Manly. Philosophical Research Society Inc; 2nd Edition, 1996, pg. 110.

- Speculative Masonry
  Yarker, John, London, 1883, pp. 563.

- Lexicon Of Freemasonry
  Mackey, Albert. George Kessinger Publishing, LLC, 1994, pg. 528.

- Encyclopedia Of Freemasonry
  Mackey, Albert. Kessinger Publishing, LLC, Virginia, 1994, pg. 528.

- Morals And Dogma Of The Ancient And Accepted Scottish Rite Of Freemasonry.

Albert Pike, Prepared For The Supreme Council of the Thirty-Third Degree (Mother Council of the World) for the Southern Jurisdiction of the United States and Published by its Authority HOUSE OF THE TEMPLE Washington, D.C. 1966 Entered according to Act of Congress, in the year 1871, by ALBERT PIKE New and Revised Edition; copyright 1950; published in 1966 The Supreme Council (Mother Council of the World) of the Inspectors General Knights Commanders of the House of the Temple of Solomon of the Thirty-third Degree of the Ancient and Accepted Scottish Rite of Freemasonry of the Southern Jurisdiction of the United States of America The Roberts Publishing Company; Washington, D.C.

- Rose Croix:
  History of the Ancient and Accepted Rite for England and Wales / A.C.F. Jackson
  Practice and Procedure for the Scottish Rite / Henry C. Clausen

- The Magnum Opus Or Great Work
  Pike, Albert; Kessinger Publishing Co.

- Legenda Magistralía
  Pike, Albert (Para uso exclusivo de los Soberanos Grandes Inspector Generales) (For the exclusive use of the Sovereign General Inspector Generals)

- Instrucciones Secretas De Los Soberanos Grandes Inspectores Generales (Para La Guía De Logias, Capítulos Y Consejos) (Secret Instructions Of The Sovereign Grand Inspector Generals)
  De la Jouquiere, Vizconde

- The Secrete Fraternities Of The Middle Ages
  Palfrey, Americo Kessinger Publishing, 1865, pp.100.

- The Book Of Ancient And Accepted Scottish Rite
  Mac-Clenanchan. Charles Thomas Scanned at Phoenixmasonry, Inc. by David Lettelier, PM and Jerry Stotler, PM, PIGM, KYCH and KCCH - May, 2006.

- The Masonic Manual
  Ashe, Jonathan. Rev. George Oliver, Kessinger Publishing, 2003, pp. 336.

- Ritual Del Soberano Gran Inspector General
  Conde Grasse Tilly

- A History Of Christianity
  Kenneth Scott, Latourrette. Christianity in a revolutionary age: a history of Christianity in the nineteenth and twentieth centuries, Volume 3, Eyre & Spottiswoode, 1961, pp. 527.

- Mere Christianity
  Lewis, C.S. HarperOne; 3rd edition, 2001, pp. 27.

- Miracles A Preliminary Study
  Lewis, C.S., Touchstone Books; 1st Touchstone Ed.edition, 1996, pp. 240.

- Nueva Evidencia Que Demanda Un Veredicto

  (Evidence That Demands A Verdict)
  McDowell, Josh. Vida; Ed. Mundo Hispano, 2004, pp. 823.

- Crazy For God:
  How I Grew Up as One of the Elect, Helped Found the Religious Right, and Lived to Take All (or Almost All) of It Back, New York: Carol & Graf Publishers, 2007.

- A Christian Manifesto
  Schaeffer, Francis. Volume 5, pp. 486.

• Babilonia Misterio Religioso (Babylon Religious Mystery)
  Woodrow, Ralph, Vida, 2008, pp. 264.

• Unmasking Freemasonry - Removing The Hoodwink
  Desenmascarando la Masonería - Removiendo la
  Venda, por Dr. Selwyn Stevens, y publicado por
  Jubilee Resources.
  P. O. Box 36-44. Wellington 6330, Nueva Zelanda.

• The Emerald Table
  Holmyard, E.J. Nature. No. 2814, Vol. 112, October 6
  1923, pp. 526.

• La Francmasoneria
  Jacq, Christian, 2 Ed. 2004, Madrid, Ediciones Martinez
  Rosa, pp. 132.

• Reglamento General Del Gran Oriente De Francia
  1885. (General Rules And Regulations Of The Great
  Orient Of France 1886)

• La Cadena De Unión Tomo Xxii Número De Marzo De
  1886. (The Chain Of Union Volume Xxii March
  1886 Number)

• Reglamentos Generales De La Masonería Escocesa,
  PARIS 1884. (RULES AND REGULATIONS OF SCOTTISH
  MASONRY, PARIS, 1884)

• Tratados Masónicos (Masonic Treatises)
  Samuel Mario Molina Del Angel

• Nineveh And Its Remains
  Llayard, A. H: London: John Murray, 1849.

NOTES

If you enjoyed reading this book, we also recommend:

Iniquity

Regions of Captivity

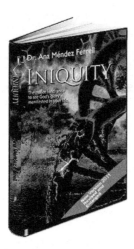

High Level Warfare

Pharmakeia

Voice of The Light Ministries

Visit our website at:

www.voiceofthelight.com

Write to:

Voice of The Light Ministries
P.O. Box 3418
Ponte Vedra, FL 32004

Follow us on **Facebook** and **Twitter**. Watch us on **Frequencies of Glory TV** and **YouTube**.

- facebook.com/VoiceoftheLight

- twitter.com/AnaMendezF

- frequenciesofglorytv.com

- youtube.com/voiceofthelight

Made in the USA
Las Vegas, NV
27 September 2021